The Tales Hunters Tell

Stories of Adventure and Inspiration

Steve Chapman

HARVEST HOUSE PUBLISHERS
EUGENE, OREGON

THE TALES HUNTERS TELL
Copyright © 2001/2014 by Steve Chapman
Published 2014 by Harvest House Publishers
Eugene, Oregon 97402
www.harvesthousepublishers.com

Library of Congress Cataloging-in-Publication Data
Chapman, Steve.
The tales hunters tell / Steve Chapman.
    pages cm
ISBN 978-0-7369-5784-7 (pbk.)
ISBN 978-0-7369-5785-4 (eBook)
1. Deer hunting—Anecdotes. 2. Conduct of life—Anecdotes. 3. Chapman, Steve. I. Title.
SK301.C5144 2014
799.2'765—dc23

                   2013043547

CONTENTS

><>·○·<><

1

We'll See Him

I looked toward the eastern skies as I exited my truck that early morning in mid-October. My arrival at the farm where I was going to bow hunt for whitetail was later than I preferred. Though the fog was thick and made it impossible to see the sky, I could tell by the ambient light that sunrise was around 15 minutes away.

I hurried as I changed into my camo, shouldered my pack, grabbed my bow, and quickstepped along the edge of a large, freshly harvested field of soybeans. I looked back toward the east and saw that the light was quickly growing. I was still at least 500 yards from where I wanted to be. As I skirted the huge field, I realized I wouldn't make it to my stand before the sun peeked over the hill behind me. I stopped walking for a moment and considered my only two options.

I could continue to follow the fencerow that led to the distant thicket where I planned to hunt. However, I knew that a late entry into the woods where my lock-on treestand was located would probably spook any deer that might already be there. My other option was to abort my trek to the treestand in the woods and go to "Plan B." Because I always keep a portable, three-legged stool on my pack, and because the slight breeze that was moving that morning would be in my face, I considered the viable alternative. I looked to my right at the fence that was just five or six yards away and thought, *No time for going any further. This place will do.*

Being as quiet as I could be, I stepped out of the field and into the knee-high weeds and small saplings that lined the fence. I knew I had to be as quick as possible. I cleared a trio of shooting lanes with my handheld trimmer. As I carefully clipped a few branches, I was grateful for the fog. *At least the mist will shield my movements from the eyes of any deer that might be in the field.*

Any disappointment I felt from being unable to follow "Plan A" that morning was wiped away when I unfolded my tri-stool and sat down. Instead of feeling defeated, I was invigorated by the challenge of hunting the wily whitetail from this impromptu ground blind. With some unplanned-but-welcomed excitement in my soul, I turned my attention to the hunt.

I scanned the few yards of the field that the dense fog allowed me to see. About 20 minutes passed, and very slowly the fog lifted. I looked into the field and slightly to my right I noticed something sort of dark in the mist 60 or 70 yards away. I watched the blurred form for about 30 seconds before I believed I detected a little bit of movement. *My eyes are playing tricks on me.* Then the brownish-gray blob, for lack of a better description, seemed to move again.

I slowly raised my binoculars and looked toward the mysterious shape. The misty cloud that still hung over the field made it hard to find the blob, but when I did my heart started pounding like it always does when I spot deer in my vicinity. "A buck! Who'd a thunk it!" I whispered, deliberately keeping my voice almost inaudible. I couldn't tell exactly how many points were on his rack, but I was able to determine that it was sizable enough to put in the "shooter" category. I noted that he was relaxed and casually feeding on the residual beans the field offered.

Another 10 minutes passed, and now the mist began to dissipate, allowing me to get a better view of the buck. He seemed to be alone. He was moving from my left to my right and had no idea I was nearby. And he didn't know I was desperately wishing he would change direction and wander toward where I was sitting.

My wish didn't come true. He continued his course toward the back corner of the field. After watching him feed and stroll along for another 15 minutes, he disappeared behind a wall of fencerow foliage. I

was tempted to stand up and take a few steps out of my hiding place—
maybe even walk to the field edge—so I could get another peek at him.
However, I opted not to make that move for fear of spooking any other
critters that might be nearby and yet unseen.

As I sat there on my stool replaying the mental video of the sighting, two distinct feelings became clear to me. On one hand, I was
pleased that I had made a hunting choice that had at least allowed me
the opportunity to see a deer. That's always a satisfying outcome for any
deer hunter even if no shots are taken. On the other hand, I felt the
sting of the likelihood that my tardy arrival to the farm had cost me a
better chance at being successful that morning.

As I went back and forth from feeling satisfied to kicking myself,
another thought came that restored some hope in the moment: *Give
the grunt call a try*. As if someone had pinched me and brought me
back to reality, I quickly unzipped my jacket, found the plastic tube,
and put it to my lips. The stillness of the morning seemed to amplify
the two-second grunt. I hoped the buck hadn't wandered out of range
of the sound.

I waited about a minute and delivered a second subtle blast on the
call before placing it inside my jacket and zipping it back up. Because
I wasn't sure if the sound had found the ears of the buck, I thought it
best to be prepared if he responded. I lifted my bow off my lap and
placed it in a horizontal position between my knees, resting the lower
wheel on my right boot. I was ready if he happened to come back into
the field and within range. The anticipation that mounted was plenty
enough to keep my spirits up.

While I waited and watched carefully to my right for any movement, I knew it would be smart to occasionally check to my left just to
make sure I wouldn't miss other deer that might come strolling down
the field. I spent a half minute or so peering to my left. When I slowly
turned my head to the right, once more looking toward the back corner of the field, I couldn't believe what I saw.

There he stood!

I felt like my entire body jumped about a foot in the air and landed
back on the stool. Thankfully, only my insides had flinched. The buck

was standing 12 to 15 yards from me. At the moment he was looking out into the field, away from my position, likely trying to find the other deer he'd heard a few minutes earlier.

I forced myself to quickly recover from the shock of the sudden reappearance of the buck and tightened my left hand on the grip of my compound bow. While I watched the deer's head for movement, I maneuvered the mechanical release strapped to my right hand to the nocking point on my string. I was totally ready to stop the process if his head turned toward me.

Hoping the buck's keen vision and attention would remain pointed toward the other side of the field, I slowly raised my bow. When I was only five inches from fully lifting it to where I could come to full draw, he turned his eyes in my direction. I froze.

Well, I tried to freeze. My fight against buck fever made it doubly hard to hold the bow still so he wouldn't notice any movement. I feared it was a lost cause until I realized I could squeeze my knees together against the lower riser to stop the entire thing from shaking.

For about a dozen seconds the buck stared right at me. I was mentally preparing to lose the battle between his wits and mine when, to my great surprise and elation, he dropped his nose to the ground and starting searching for more breakfast. When he took a couple more steps to my left, I took the opportunity to get to full draw.

The soft material of my camo jacket didn't make a sound as I struggled against the tightness of the bow string. About the time I reached the point where the bow's draw weight went from 58 pounds to 25 pounds or so, the buck looked up again. He instantly turned his head toward the movement he'd seen out of his peripheral vision—my arm motions. But it was too late for him. His vitals were already covered by the round, red, 15-yard pin on my sights.

The arrow took off like a missile! In an instant it passed through the buck and torpedoed into the dirt somewhere beyond him. He jumped and ran straight across the field, probably headed to where he'd entered it from the other side. About halfway across, I saw him stumble and then crash into the moist dirt. Within seconds he passed from this life and into my book of treasured memories.

I sat on the stool feeling quite stunned by what had taken place. Needless to say, the unplanned stand choice, the unexpected sighting, the quick choice to try the grunt call, and the unpredicted outcome of the morning hunt were very pleasing details to think about. I decided to sit for a few minutes and bask in the glow of success. To this day that glow hasn't lost its shine. I still enjoy recalling every little moment of that morning. And, as it often happens, the more I think about a particular hunt, the more likely it is that I'll discover a connection between something that took place during the experience and something I've read in the Scriptures. This hunt was no exception, and what I saw was helpful to me. Perhaps you'll also see some value in it.

When I first realized that the nearly colorless, fog-distorted blob that I saw through my binoculars was a buck, my heart leaped with excitement. The thrill remained until I could no longer see him because he disappeared behind some foliage. As joyous as the feeling was that came with having seen him, the opposite is how disappointing it felt to assume I'd never see him again. It was this pendulum swing of emotion that I thought about again when I read John 16.

In this passage, Jesus warned His disciples about what was about to happen as the time of His crucifixion was approaching. He said, "A little while, and you will no longer see Me; and again a little while, and you will see Me" (verse 16). The disciples didn't totally understand their Master's statement and questioned what He meant by "a little while." Apparently they had a rousing discussion about it in Jesus' presence because He said to them, "Are you deliberating together about this, that I said, 'A little while, and you will not see Me, and again a little while, and you will see Me'?" (verse 19).

Knowing that His disciples were troubled by the mere thought of Him not being with them even for a little while, Jesus offered them some comfort with His next words:

> Truly, truly, I say to you, that you will weep and lament, but
> the world will rejoice; you will grieve, but your grief will
> be turned into joy. Whenever a woman is in labor she has
> pain, because her hour has come; but when she gives birth

to the child, she no longer remembers the anguish because of the joy that a child has been born into the world. Therefore you too have grief now; but I will see you again, and your heart will rejoice, and no one will take your joy away from you (John 16:20-22).

In time, after the death of Jesus and His glorious resurrection that followed, the disciples fully understood what the Lord meant by "and again a little while, and you will see Me." What abundant joy they must have felt when Christ once again appeared alive in front of them the third day after His death on the cross. This is a joy time has not erased.

Christ's statement recorded in John 16 was obviously about the fact that He would be crucified and buried, thus being out of the disciples' sight for a short while. But when He was raised from the dead, He appeared before them again. However, His words go beyond that specific point in time. In fact, His words bring hope to countless hearts today, including mine. Those of us who have seen Jesus Christ through eyes of faith and feel the joy of the reality of His presence through the Holy Spirit in our lives cling to Jesus' words, "And again a little while, and you will see Me."

We believe that someday the One we see through faith will appear again! In that moment we will "see Him just as He is" (1 John 3:2). Yet, to be candid, just like the disciples felt an acute sorrow that Jesus was out of their sight even for a while, there are times when holding to the hope of seeing Him again is a challenge for those of us who follow Him today. It's not easy to maintain a high level of anticipation for His return when there's so much loss, sorrow, doubt, and dread in our world.

In the face of that challenge, I'm encouraged to recall how I sat that morning on my tri-stool at the edge of that soybean field feeling down that the buck had disappeared...but still holding on to the tiny hope that he'd "heard my cry" when I used the grunt call and I would see him again. In a similar, yet far more important way, the Lord hears the call of my heart as I wait at life's field edge. I know He will appear again! This anticipation keeps me engaged in the hunt to become more like Him and makes the time pass more joyfully.

We'll See Him Again

Oh, what a morning it surely will be
When our eyes of flesh are blessed to see
The One who till now has only been known
Through what we have seen by faith alone

The sorrow and sadness that have hidden the view
Of His glorious form from me and from you
Will lift like a fog from life's troubled field
And His marvelous presence will be revealed

Then the joy that once seemed so far away
Will enter our hearts, and it will stay
And until that morning when our sorrows will end
We can trust in a while we'll see Him again [1]

2

I Saw It on My Own!

Tim had just turned 13 years old when his mother, Cathy, called me a couple of weeks before gun season opened for deer in our area. Annie and I had known the family for four years or so, and Cathy was well aware that I was an avid hunter.

"Mr. Steve," she said, using the uniquely Southern greeting she always did, "could I ask a huge favor of you?"

"Sure, Cathy, fire away."

Her tone was apologetic as she spoke. "Tim has been bugging us about letting him go hunting. He's been through the state-required hunter's safety course, but his dad and I are so busy with work and raising these kids that neither one of us can take him to the woods. I was wondering if you'd be willing to let him tag along with you sometime this year."

The moment I heard Cathy's request, the rush of excitement made me smile. One opportunity that a mature deer hunter won't pass up is helping newbies fill their tags for the first time. There's a satisfying feeling that comes with seeing new hunters' eyes widen at the sight of an incoming deer and hearing their breathing get progressively heavier as the creature comes within range. It's a thrill to watch their hands shake as they try desperately to calm their nerves enough to hold their guns steady so they can take accurate shots.

Perhaps the reason we elders enjoy observing the flustered behaviors of new hunters is that it brings back sweet memories of our own introductions to the taste of adrenaline pie when it's served up in the hunter's woods. We never tire of remembering those unforgettable moments, and the chance to relive them through a youngster is probably a main reason we are "Johnny on the spot" when it comes to letting a newbie go with us.

I didn't hesitate to answer Cathy's request. "Absolutely! I'd be happy to take your young Nimrod to a deer stand. I have a place I think might yield some good results for him. I'll call you back with some dates."

Before we ended our phone conversation, Cathy told me that Tim was reading everything he could get his hands on about deer hunting. Plus his dad had purchased a few videos for him to watch so he could learn some "tricks of the trail."

I could only imagine how tough it was for Tim to be so wildly stimulated by the hunting magazine articles and films of hunters bagging one big buck after another. I figured by the time the next two weeks passed he'd be pawing at the ground, ready to run to my chosen deer hunting area. I was right!

The first chance I had to take Tim hunting for a few hours was on the afternoon of a school day. His parents agreed to let him leave school early so we could be in the woods by two o'clock. When I pulled into the driveway of his home to pick him up just after one, he was standing on the porch wearing his newly purchased camo pants, shirt, and hat. He had his .243 rifle cased and ready to load into the truck. I've never seen a young man more eager to head to the woods than "Mr. Tim."

As we drove to the farm where we'd spend the rest of the day, I offered some insights I was sure would be useful for a new hunter. Tim was very attentive.

"Your mama told me you've been reading up on deer hunting," I said. "Sounds like you haven't missed a page of the magazines you have. It was smart of you to realize you should learn all you can about hunting. You can never get too much information when it comes to things you need to know to outwit a whitetail. They definitely have the advantage."

As though the dam had broken that held back all the tips about deer hunting I'd gathered during the previous 40 years, I rambled on and on. Tim didn't seem to mind as I discussed whitetail traits, including how their ears, eyes, and noses are a hundred times better than humans' and how they seem to have a sixth sense when it comes to detecting danger.

For the next 20 minutes Tim couldn't get a word in as I deposited more of my hard-earned hunting and woods knowledge into his memory banks. The last thing I told him before we arrived at the farm was a tip about one of the toughest challenges he'd face that day. I put it in that category because it was the biggest challenge for me when I was a young teenager on a deer stand.

"Tim, we'll be sitting on the ground this evening instead of in a treestand. For that reason, we can't move around a lot. In fact, any movement we make has to be very, *very* slow. The eyes of a deer will catch the slightest unusual motion. I won't be able to raise my arm to point to where a deer is. If I see one and you don't, I'll whisper to help you spot it, but that'll be about all I can do."

The way Tim leaned forward in his seat told me he was chomping at the bit to experience everything I'd talked about. As I parked the truck I had one more thing to say before we opened the doors and headed out.

"I'll remind you about this again after we settle in where we'll be hunting, but if I see a deer and you don't, I'll *whisper* its location to you. When you whisper back, don't turn your head. Even that tiny movement might get us busted. Got it?"

"Yes, sir, Mr. Steve!"

Fifteen minutes later I was scraping the leaves away on the ground to make a quiet place for us to sit under a wide oak tree. The old oak stood along a fencerow at the edge of a good-sized, rectangular field. It was about 75 yards to the opposite side, where I fully expected the deer to enter for their evening meal. Facing the field with our backs leaning against the huge trunk, I quietly gave Tim a heads-up about what might happen.

"As you can see, over on the other side is a hill that drops down into this field we're watching. That hillside is one of the favorite places that deer love to bed during the day. When they get up to feed later on this afternoon, they'll browse inside the woods on acorns until about 30 minutes or so before dark. Then, if I'm right, they'll leave the woods and walk into the open field. That's when you might get a chance at taking one of them."

Tim shivered with anticipation. He was so excited I wasn't sure if he was going to be able to sit still. I thought maybe a little more coaching would help calm him a little.

"It's pretty quiet this evening since the wind is down. That's in our favor for two reasons. First, the wind will not carry our human scent to the other side of the field. Second, because the leaves are so dry we might be able to hear them coming off the hill. You'll love that part. The sound of moving deer is music to a hunter's ears. But keep in mind that if we hear some leaves crunching it might not be deer. It could be squirrels. They make a different sound. I'll point out the difference if we hear both."

I paused and took a long breath. I decided to resist the urge to tell Mr. Tim everything else I knew and save some for later. "Now it's time to just watch and listen."

I was quite impressed with how still Tim sat and eyed the area. Just like I'd requested, when he moved his head to look up and down the field he did it very slowly. His knees had been raised for about 20 minutes, the heels of his boots tucked up next to his behind. It was a position that even a flexible teenager can't endure for a long period of time.

"Mr. Steve," he whispered, "may I put my legs on the ground?"

"Yes, but let me check around us first."

As I visually scanned the area I whispered, "Here's a tip. When you're hunting on the ground, it's always good to be as sure as you can that nothing is watching before you make major body adjustments. And clearing away the dry leaves around where you're sitting or standing is also good 'cause when you move you won't make noises the deer can hear." Satisfied no deer were watching, I nodded at Tim and whispered, "Go ahead."

Tim got comfortable, and for the next 45 minutes we quietly watched, and listened, and occasionally talked in low tones about some of the articles he'd read in hunting magazines and what he'd seen in some videos.

"What's one of the favorite things you read or saw?" I asked.

Tim slowly turned his face toward me and grinned. He told me about a story written by a hunter who, by himself, went West to hunt elk. Tim was intrigued by the idea of going it alone into the backcountry with just a bow, a backpack, a one-man tent, and a week's worth of supplies. "Someday I want to do what that guy did!"

I returned a wide grin as Tim whispered more details of his fantasy. I could hear my own heart in his words. Around 14 years of age I too had dreamed about the same thing as I read about other hunters' adventures in magazines such as *Fur, Fish & Game* and *Outdoor Life*. It was sheer joy to hear the echo of that yearning in Tim's voice. I was just about to tell Tim about my long-time dream of a one-man elk hunt when I noticed some movement on the other side of the field. Slowly I glanced at my watch and then looked at my hunting partner.

"Tim, that 'magic' hour of 4:30 has arrived, and I think the deer have too. Look straight across the field and find that large cedar that's shaped like an upside down teardrop. See it?"

"The really dark-green tree?" Tim was suddenly so excited his voice went in and out of a whisper.

"Yes, that's the one. Now, to the right of it is a much shorter cedar. Between the big one and the small one, there's a fence post. See it?"

"Yes, sir."

"There's a deer standing on the other side of that post. See it?"

"No, sir."

Tim had his legs flat on the ground, which meant he would have no rest for his gun if he needed to take good solid aim and shoot.

"While the deer is still back in the woods, slowly raise your knees so you can rest your gun on one of them for a shot. I'll watch the deer. If it looks nervous, I'll tell you to stop."

Tim followed my instructions and moved slowly. When he was finally in position, I turned his attention back to finding the deer that was still standing beyond the fence.

"Do you see the deer yet?"

"No, sir. Is he still where he was?" Tim didn't turn his head toward me to answer. He was doing great.

"Yes. It hasn't moved. It might be a doe. Whatever it is, it's almost like it's waiting until it gets a little closer to evening before coming out into the field. Deer are smart that way. That's why they live long enough to get big. Do you see it yet?"

"No, sir."

I'd forgotten about color identification! "Tim, did you notice that the fence post is a really light-gray color?"

"Uh huh."

"Okay, now notice that the color of the woods *beyond* the post is somewhere between a light and dark brown."

"Yes, sir."

"That splotch of color in the middle is the fur of a deer. It's standing broadside with its head to the left. If you follow that splotch to the top, you'll make out the shape of the back. It has a slight curve in it, sort of like a horse's back does."

"Oh! I see it! I see it! Oh, man, I can see it! How did you find that?"

The question was sweet to hear. So were the footsteps of more deer coming down the hillside as I quietly explained to Tim how to pick out the well-camouflaged deer.

"That area beyond that fence post was a dark hole a few minutes ago. When I saw that it had filled with color, it got my attention."

I seized the moment and offered another tip. "When I first get to where I'm going to hunt, I study the area very carefully. I memorize as many of the shapes and tones of color as I can. Then if something changes, it's easier for me to recognize it. Many times I've spotted deer that way. Now, keep watching and see if you can spot more deer coming down the hill. Can you hear them?"

"Not yet," Tim said, sounding concerned.

"Listen for soft crunches. Deer usually walk steadily, so their pace doesn't sound flighty. Squirrels scamper across the leaves, but deer steps are regular and sound sort of humanlike."

Tim turned his head slightly to listen closely for walking deer. His whisper was a bit louder when he spoke. "I do hear them now! Oh…I think I see another deer! It's beyond the next fence post, to the right of the one we've been looking at. Yes! I see it. I found it all by myself! Do you see it?"

"I do! It's brown like the other one. I can make out the shape of the head, and its ears appear to be tall. Looks like a doe to me."

I could hear Tim's feeling of satisfaction in the way he whispered, "Wow! I can't believe I found it on my own just the way you did the first one. This is so cool."

It took 15 long minutes before five deer walked out into the field. And as the sun was setting, I was teaching a youngster how to field dress his deer. The 95-pound doe was a real trophy—as good to both of us as a 12-point buck would have been.

Besides the joy of helping a newbie get his first kill and the celebration that followed, there's one other thrilling memory I especially enjoy recalling about the hunt. It was a great moment when I heard him say, "I found it all by myself!" As far as I'm concerned, it was the highest compliment he could have given me. His words reminded me of what Jesus said to the woman at the well. The event is highlighted in the book of John, chapter 4.

When this woman encountered Jesus just outside of her town at Jacob's well, she learned that she'd met the One who would introduce her to the water that would forever quench her spiritual thirst. She also learned that He found her acceptable even though He knew she was a Samaritan (most Jews of that time detested Samaritans) and was aware of all that she'd done. She was so moved by Him that she went back to town and told the men about Jesus. Then she said, "Come, see a man who told me all the things that I have done" (John 4:29).

Because of her words, the men responded and went to hear Jesus. What they said to her after listening to Jesus was the highest compliment that can be paid to anyone who, like the Samaritan woman, is a witness or evangelist for Christ. They said to her, "It is no longer because of what you said that we believe, for we have heard for ourselves and know that this One is indeed the Savior of the world" (verse 42).

Hearing Tim, my hunting student, say that he saw the deer on his own was indeed a huge thrill for me. But it's miniscule compared to the immense joy the Samaritan woman must have felt when she helped the people of her town recognize for themselves the Savior of the world. Without a doubt, their saying, "We have heard for ourselves and know" was the highest honor that she could imagine! And it's an honor that is available to all of us who have seen and acknowledged who Jesus is through eyes of faith and are willing to introduce Him to others.

> *[Jesus said,] "My prayer is not for them alone. I pray also for those who will believe in me through their message"* (John 17:20 NIV).

3

Unpredictable

There are some things in this world that are simply unpredictable. For example, who can really know in advance the way of a golf ball? I certainly can't. I would never have guessed what happened several years ago on a course in our area.

I was playing in a threesome, and we reached a tee box that faced an elevated, par-three green. Like all the tee shots before, I was last in the sequence to hit. I couldn't see the surface of the green, but the very top of the flag was showing. I addressed the ball and said, "Do right by me, baby!" Then, following such a tender show of affection for the little white, dimpled sphere, I proceeded to violently abuse it with my 9 iron.

Much to my amazement, the club did something very unusual. It worked! The ball flew straight and high and looked like it landed on the green! I couldn't wait to get to the "dance floor" and see how close I'd gotten to the pin.

Though they seemed quite shocked (and maybe a little jealous), my friends congratulated me as we made the climb from the tee box to the green. When we got there, I saw two golf balls. One was 15 feet from the hole; the other at least 40 feet away.

Hoping my shot landed closest to the flag I walked over and checked the markings on the ball. Sadly, it wasn't. The second ball was identified by its owner. That meant mine had apparently rolled off the backside of the putting surface. Sorely disappointed, I searched for it. As I passed by the hole, I happened to look down. I stopped dead in my tracks and stared. I couldn't believe it! I bent over and looked closely. "Hey, guys! Check this out!" I yelled.

I reached into the cup and pulled out my one-and-only "hole in one" ball. Though I didn't get to enjoy the thrill of seeing it land on the green and roll into the cup, I admit that I got a ton of enjoyment out of reminding my buddies about that ace for the rest of the round…and the weeks and months to come.

I never would have stood on the tee and predicted my shot would go into the hole! For a fleeting moment I wondered if there might be a place for me on the PGA tour. As I smiled at the thought, I remembered another thing I like to do much more. Although it does have some things in common with golf, what I really love is hunting. And that sport has me looking for something too.

While there are some things about hunting that can be accurately foretold, such as an arrow's flight (with practice), wind direction, and the time the sun rises, there are other aspects that can't be predicted. For instance, which direction deer will come from when I'm in a stand, when another hunter might stalk through the area, and when a pack of dogs might come through and clear the woods of my hope to see deer.

Of the many unpredictable things that have happened while hunting, one of the most intriguing involved a doe during archery season. I was in a treestand with my traditional bow. I'd never bagged a deer while shooting with a recurve. I'd put in a lot of practice, so I felt I was ready for the challenge. Around 8:30 in the morning, my chance came.

A mature doe walked under the big oak I was in and began browsing on the fallen acorns. The conditions were in my favor. With the wind in my face and foliage that was still on the tree hiding my silhouette, I was able to move without being detected. I waited for the right moment, pulled the string, took aim, and let go. I was amazed at how quiet the bow was for the 14-yard shot. I was stunned, however, when the arrow flew right over the doe's back. She flinched just a little when the arrow hit the dirt near her with a soft thud. She looked at the arrow for a second or two and then continued feeding.

I figured she must have thought the arrow was a branch that had fallen from the tree. Surprised that she didn't run off, I very slowly and carefully took another arrow from the quiver that hung on a nail next to me. I got it on the string and came to full draw again. This shot was about the same distance as the first one. This time the arrow flew right underneath her belly. Once again the quietness of the bow didn't spook her, although this second "stick" made her jump slightly. As before, she chose to ignore it and kept enjoying her breakfast.

By the time I nocked my third arrow, she was 20 or so yards away— still close enough for another try. And that's what it was—a try. The arrow fell short of the target and buried itself in the dirt near her. Because of the less downward angle of flight, the arrow hit the ground and dirt and leaves flew up around it. The impact surprised the doe enough to make her react more noticeably, but she didn't run away. Instead, she walked back toward the tree.

On her way back to where she was when I took the first shot, she stopped and smelled my second arrow. Although I'm always careful about hiding my human scent, I was sure she would smell the odor from my hands touching it as she nosed the orange-and-black fletching. She studied the wooden shaft for a few seconds before going back to browsing for acorns.

I put the fourth of my four arrows on my string. When I released it, it sailed over her back. I couldn't believe how inept I was with my shooting. I stood in the stand shaking my head in disbelief. I considered the idea of climbing down, retrieving my arrows, and trying four more shots. I figured the way the doe was acting, my descent from the stand wouldn't bother her.

It wasn't easy to admit that I'd been defeated by my lack of traditional archery talent. I resolved to go back to the practice range and get better at it so I wouldn't be guilty of delivering an unmercifully inaccurate shot the next time I took the bow to the stand.

As I stood there, I considered how totally surprised I'd been by the doe's unpredictable response to a sudden, unidentifiable sound. Any other time, my first errant shot would have sent her running to the other side of the county. I whispered as she finally wandered away from the tree I was in and got out of range, "Wassup with her?" I chalked it up to a female exercising her prerogative, which is basically what I do when my sweet wife has entertained (for lack of a better word) me with reactions I would never have predicted. I'll share two of them with you because they left me scratching my head and I'm sure you can relate.

Annie and I were scheduled to join some friends at a party across town, but we couldn't ride together due to the need to go in different directions afterward. We decided Annie would follow me in her car since I had the map. We each had cell phones that we'd just gotten, so we agreed to use them if we got separated.

Twenty-five minutes later I pulled up in front of the house where our friends were gathering and got out of the car. I looked down the road to see if Annie was coming, but I didn't see her. I realized the last time I'd seen her was a couple of turns back. I'd been busy looking at the map and making turns and hadn't realized we'd gotten separated.

I stood in the front yard by the curb of the house watching and hoping I'd see her turn onto the street where I was. I was sure my cell phone would ring any second so I could give her directions or at least go to where she was. Five minutes turned into eight, then ten, and still no call. I got back into my car to go find her. When I got to the corner where I was sure I'd last seen her, she was arriving from a different direction.

Our gazes connected. I could see that she was quite miffed. I turned my car around, and she drove behind me and followed me to the party. When we parked at the curb and exited our vehicles, we had a verbal exchange that I won't forget. Her share of words was delivered with as much restraint as my very upset wife could muster.

"Why on earth didn't you answer your phone? I called it a dozen times, and you didn't answer!"

"It never rang, babe," I said, a bit puzzled. Our phones weren't set up for speed dial, and I imagined her stopping every 300 yards and punching in the numbers. It was no wonder she was flustered!

"Well, I called and called and started circling the streets. If you hadn't come and looked for me, I'd probably never be seen again. I can't believe you didn't answer your phone!"

Then it dawned on me to ask a question—one that I wasn't totally sure would be smart to put out there. But curiosity got the best of me. "What number did you dial?"

She rattled off the number.

I stared at her but didn't say anything.

"What?" she sputtered as she threw her phone into her purse.

I almost hated to respond, but I did because she asked. I smiled as I said it, hoping to soften the blow.

"That's not my number."

What she said next is a statement no man alive would ever anticipate. With her hand on her hip, which just about every husband knows is a sign of impending doom, she said, "You should have answered it anyway!"

I could have made a thousand guesses at what she would say when she found out she was calling the wrong number and not even gotten close to getting it right. Wisely, I kept quiet and pondered what I'd just heard. It was certainly plenty to think about.

The second story about what Annie said is just as scary…er…I mean unforgettable.

We were traveling by air one weekend to three different cities to perform concerts. (Annie and I are musicians.) Two of the events were completed, and by the time we got to the airport for our third day of flying, we were both worn out. To make matters worse, the traffic tie-up on the drive to the terminal caused us to get to the airport much later than we'd planned.

We hurried through the return of the rental car, ran with our luggage from the rental car shuttle to the check-in counter, begged them to rush us through the sign-in, and then took off to get to security. The line at security was longer than we hoped, and we bit our nails as we moved like honey on a winter day through the process. Finally we got on the other side of the security checkpoint, took off sprinting, and got to the gate just as they were about to close the door of the plane.

Drenched with sweat and frazzled by the craziness of the morning, we plopped down in our seats and buckled up. Thankfully the flight took off on time. Our relief was short lived, however, when the pilot announced that the weather at our connecting city wasn't good. When the lead flight attendant announced that all passengers who were scheduled on a connecting flight would need to be released from the plane first, we knew it was going to be a tight connection. Now we were back to biting our nails. We couldn't miss the next flight and still make it to the event where around 1000 people were expected to attend.

As we sat in our seats, we tried to calm ourselves with something other than worrying. Annie searched the seat pocket in front of her to get something to read. That's when I heard her gasp. I turned to her quickly. "What's wrong?"

"Look at this!" She held up some papers. "These are our boarding passes for our next flight! I don't for the life of me remember putting them in the seat pocket. Oh my word! If I hadn't found these, we would have run off this plane and been held up at the connecting gate. And as tight as the schedule's gonna be, we would have missed our next flight."

I wanted to thank her for discovering the passes and skirting such an unwanted disaster. "Wow! I'm glad you found the tickets, babe. You saved us from a heap of trouble!"

What she said next could have brought the plane down. For sure it caused my psyche to crash. Once again, I could have guessed a thousand—no, a million—times and never predicted what I heard.

My sweet wife said, "Well, you know if we'd have gotten off this plane without these passes and missed our next flight, it would have been your fault anyway."

I looked at her expecting to see a mischievous grin, but it wasn't there. She was serious! And that's the part that I found especially chilling.

The words she said while standing in the front yard of the house where the party was held and the ones in the airplane are logged away in my brain in the file cabinet labeled, "Wassup with that?" I suppose as long as I live I'll never understand the theory or the thinking behind either statement, but I'm gonna keep trying. Why? Because I'm biblically commanded to. My orders are found in 1 Peter 3:7: "You husbands...live with your wives in an understanding way."

What a challenging command to put on us married guys, especially when we hear disturbing quips like "There are two ways to argue successfully with a woman, but neither of them work" and "There are two things about a woman every man ought to know, but nobody knows what they are." Men laugh at these adages, but we do it nervously. At least I do because of the truth that's in them. Most of us are aware that we have our work cut out for us when it comes to understanding the women God gave us.

As challenging as women can be at times, could it be their unpredictableness—the mystery of how their minds work, the way they reason, and how they respond to things we do or say—is God's way of keeping us interested in them? Surely He knew that just like we'd consider the game of golf boring if we knew exactly where every shot was going to end up or, in hunting, the mystique of the chase would wane if we knew exactly where deer were going to appear and what they would do, we'd lose interest in our wives if we thought we had them all figured out.

So, if you're a married man (or about to be married) and a hunter, the next time you're in the woods watching a doe do something completely unexpected and it's totally messing with your brain, remember to thank God for the reminder to never stop trying to understand your wife. It's a great way to love her and honor the One who created her for you.

4

Me & Mel

With no wind moving inside the canopy of trees where I sat, everything in the woods was at a quiet calm. The stillness made it extra easy to see the slightest movement. I was set up 60 yards from the edge of a thicket that was dense with late-September foliage. As I stared at the wall of brush, I felt my eyes widen when I saw the momentary wobble of one limb on a single sapling. It had my full attention.

I kept looking, waiting for more motion. It was probably another 30 seconds before it happened again. When it did, my confidence that a deer was present skyrocketed. Without hesitating or taking my eyes off that section of woods, I stood up and got ready to take a shot with my compound bow. In another minute I saw the familiar brown fur that covers a whitetail body. I was seeing only the midsection of the animal, so I wasn't yet sure if it was a buck or doe. I continued to watch and wait. Being 15 feet above the ground on my portable stand and with the wind down, I knew the advantage was mine. All I had to do was be patient.

I assumed the deer had been resting all day in the security of the leafy bedroom the thicket provided. I was the uninvited guest sitting in the dining room where the woods were open and peppered with tall white and red oaks. The yield of acorns was plentiful, and I was sure the waking deer would be walking into the eating room well before the woods would be darkened by the setting sun. I was, to say the least, pumped.

Finally, as though opening its bedroom door and walking straight to the dinner table, the deer, a solitary and decent-sized buck, stepped out of the thicket and into the openness of the big woods. He was doing exactly what I'd hoped—feeding on the fruit of the oaks while slowly making his way to the soybean field behind me. The way I had it figured, if he kept on course it would take him 10 to 15 minutes to come by me…on my right about 18 yards away.

I needed to turn my body to accommodate my right-handed shot, so I went ahead and carefully made the turn. The buck was still 40 yards away and barely moving forward. I was glad to have completed the adjustment without making noise. The slightest unusual sound in the stillness of the evening would have sent the deer bounding back into the thicket.

With 20 more yards for the deer to cover before it was time to come to full draw, I slowly moved my right hand to the nocking point on the string. I looked down to make sure I was putting the jaws of my release around the string in the right place. That's when I heard a noise coming from my left. It sounded like a tree limb snapped by something big.

Curiosity got the best of me. I slowly turned my head to find the source of the noise. I saw nothing at first as I scanned the open timber. I continued searching, all the while wondering if the buck to my right was moving. I started to turn my focus back to the buck when I heard another sound. It was distinct enough to keep me searching for a few extra seconds. I hoped the buck on my right was still taking his time as he browsed.

There was a reason for my willingness to turn my attention to the new sound coming from my left. I knew there were other bucks on the farm that exceeded the size of the buck on my right. As I transferred my full attention to the search for what I hoped was something bigger, I had a momentary, nagging suspicion that it wasn't a good idea to ignore the "sure thing" that was feeding nearby. But I waited anyway. "Aha!" I whispered to myself when another patch of brown fur appeared just inside the thicket. I congratulated myself for knowing enough about deer hunting to successfully recognize the telltale sound of moving deer. The anticipation for what size the newcomer might be was overwhelming. Finally it stepped out of the heavy foliage and into the open woods. It was a young, scrawny doe…and it too appeared to be alone.

I could feel my shoulders droop under the weight of disappointment. But the doldrums disappeared quickly when I remembered the incoming buck to my right. He was a respectable eight point (a 4 x 4 or four point for you westerners). As I turned my head in his direction to see how much he'd moved, I saw only trees around me. I can't explain how I didn't hear a single step the buck took as he left, but he was gone. Where he went and why are still mysteries to me.

I couldn't believe it! I'd turned my eyes away from the buck for what I thought was a brief moment, but obviously it was enough time for him to quietly walk out of my life. All that was left in the dining room was a skinny, hungry young girl deer that was much too young for taking.

When the evening ended, the only thing I took from the woods was my climbing stand, my unexercised bow and full quiver, and some wounds to my ego to lick. Eventually something good came from the experience. I discovered a connection between what happened that day and something that happened a few months later following an event I attended at a large church in Hendersonville, Tennessee.

Annie and I got a call from our son, Nathan, who is in the music business in Nashville. His growing influence as a successful, Grammy-winning producer includes some perks not afforded to many folks. One of them was an expanding list of friends who were also successful and had lots of connections to well-known music industry figures.

Back in early 2004, when production for the movie *The Passion of the Christ* was nearing completion, there were several prerelease screenings planned in cities across the nation. Many of the screenings were held in churches, and local leaders were invited. I assumed the purpose for involving the Christian community was to help fill theater seats on opening day of the official release of the movie. Nashville was chosen for a screening, and the list of special invitees included more than influential church leaders. Several music celebrities were asked to be there as well.

A well-known artist in the country and blue grass genre who is an outspoken Christian accepted the responsibility of inviting some music celebrities in the area. Because our son was acquainted with him and they shared common ground in terms of their faith, Nathan was among the invitees to the screening. He was told he could bring three people as his guests. Along with his wife, Nathan asked Annie and me to attend.

It's hard to describe how excited we were to get to go to the special screening of a Hollywood movie. When we walked into the church sanctuary that was filled with more than 1000 influential local church leaders and music celebrities, we felt like royalty.

The movie began with none of the usual visual cinematic fanfare that is typically seen in theaters. There were no titles, no credits, no company logos, and very little music. It simply started with the opening scene of the film. Though there were elements of the movie that were yet to be completed in the post-filming stage of the process, the version we saw was profoundly moving.

When the last scene faded it was amazing how quiet the sanctuary was. We were collectively stunned by the impact we felt from watching such a realistic representation of the crucifixion of Christ, and by the incredibly inspiring way the resurrection was depicted. When the screen faded to complete black, it was as though no one could breathe. I've never heard such an absence of sound in a room filled with so many people.

As I sat in my aisle seat in a pew about 20 rows back from the pulpit, my emotions were drenched with deep gratitude for what Christ had gone through for the sake of my redemption. I closed my eyes and felt my spirit simultaneously crying out in agony about Jesus' death and singing praise to Him for enduring it and being my risen Savior.

The uncommon stillness in the room seemed to last forever. Finally I took a breath, but I did so as quietly as I could. I didn't want to disturb the sacredness of the silence. I wondered how many others were doing the same. Then I heard a slight noise behind me and to my right. It sounded like shuffling footsteps. If the room hadn't been so quiet, I'm not sure I would have heard it.

Wondering who would be so rude and uncaring to destroy such a moment by getting up and walking, I opened my eyes and looked to my right. I caught the movement of someone walking up the aisle. I turned my head a little more toward the back of the sanctuary to make out the face. When I saw him, I had to do everything I could not to audibly gasp. It was the movie's director, Mel Gibson!

In that instant all the other times I'd seen that face flashed across my mind. I saw quick pieces of scenes from *Braveheart, The Patriot, Signs, Conspiracy Theory,* and a few others. The one who had so skillfully entertained me and millions of others with his unique acting ability was about to pass within a mere three feet of where I sat. I was, to admit the obvious, star-struck.

I was among only a few who noticed who was moving in the room. Admittedly, we didn't waste any time in spreading the word. Elbows flew faster than arrows, and by the time he reached the stage, took a seat on a stool, and was given a handheld microphone for speaking, everyone was on their feet offering a standing ovation. It was not only a spontaneous response to such an unexpected guest, but also a rousing show of support for directing and taking part in producing such an incredible movie. All of us could hardly wait to hear what he had to say.

For the next 30 minutes we listened to Mr. Gibson speak about the filming. His comments were on interesting topics such as cast selection, technical challenges, and plans for the music that would accompany the finished version. The evening ended with another standing ovation for the film and its director.

After the crowd was dismissed, Annie and I thanked Nathan profusely for inviting us to the event. We headed home, and the drive back to our house was a half-hour filled with nonstop conversation about the experience.

When I went to bed that night and turned out the light beside me, I was still reeling emotionally from the screening. I replayed nearly everything that had happened, from arriving at the church and seeing such an impressive collection of well-known music people and church leaders to being overwhelmed by the quality of the movie. I also thought about being so physically close to a famous actor.

Then something happened as I stared into the darkness that I won't forget. As if a spotlight were turned on in my memory of the evening, the only area it showed was around me at the end of the pew and Mel Gibson in the aisle. I imagined myself off to the side watching the lit scene. I saw the puzzled look on my face when I heard the shuffling of feet, and I watched my head turn to the right and then on around to look behind me to see who it was. I could see how Mr. Gibson deliberately walked as quietly as possible to avoid distracting others and being noticed. He had his left hand on his chin, perhaps to partially cover his face in hopes he wouldn't be recognized until he was ready.

From that aisle scene, the spotlight immediately focused on Mr. Gibson sitting down on the stool on the stage. I noticed how he seemed so humbly regretful that his unexpected appearance may have stolen the moment from the far more important Person featured in the movie. His reserved demeanor was endearing.

Then the spotlight instantly flashed back to me in the aisle seat looking at Mel as he passed within arm's reach. I noticed my expression when I realized who he was. My wide-eyed ogling was rather comical at first, but then I felt a chill as I realized what had really happened. In one instant, just after the movie ended at the screening, I was literally baptized in thanks, praise, and worship of the crucified-yet-living Christ. The movie had accomplished its purpose in my heart, and my full, undivided focus was on my Savior and the Savior of the world. Nothing else in the universe mattered to me—and I mean nothing. My spirit would have been totally content if that moment never ended. It was a glorious time of unbridled worship.

In the next instant, however, the pendulum of my attention and my affection swung wildly from the risen Christ to Mel Gibson. It was a swing that I'm confident Mel didn't intend. I'm sure he would be disappointed to know that it did. Yet it happened.

As I lay awake processing the reality that I had so easily shifted my focus…or should I say my worship…from the victorious Christ to a frail human, I felt sad. I'd traded the eternal "sure thing" for the temporal "passing thing." It was a lot like what happened when I turned my focus away from the eight-point buck and focused on what turned out to be a scrawny doe.

Mr. Gibson may never know about the struggle with focus I dealt with at the Nashville screening of his movie *The Passion of the Christ*, but I'm confident the Lord knew about it. And I'm grateful for the comfort of knowing that He has forgiven me for it. He understands that I'm weak enough to let that happen from time to time. As a result of the "me and Mel" experience, I've set a goal to not let my worship ever again shift from Christ to anyone else or, for that matter, anything else. Whether it's a celebrity, a trophy of some kind (including deer), money, fame, influence, or even worry, I purpose to do what Hebrews 12:1-2 instructs:

> Let us also lay aside every encumbrance and the sin which so easily entangles us, and let us run with endurance the race that is set before us, fixing our eyes on Jesus, the author and perfecter of faith, who for the joy set before Him endured the cross, despising the shame, and has sat down at the right hand of the throne of God.

I want to keep my eyes "fixed on Jesus, on whom our faith depends from beginning to end" (Hebrews 12:2 GNT). One thing is for certain. The next time I'm in a treestand and my attention is torn between two deer, I'll remember the "me and Mel" moment. I hope you will too. Maybe it'll help us both leave the woods with something to show for our efforts.

5

Tangled Web

Deer hunting in early archery season in our neck of the timber means being in the woods while the insects are still active. Consequently, I've had lots of creepy-crawly things appear in my stand area that get my attention. Many of them, like harmless black ants or grasshoppers, show up and I simply ignore them. But, on occasion, one of my least favored of all multi-legged creatures invades my space—the spider.

The scientific name of the pest is *araneae*. In my opinion, the name sounds much too innocent. I wonder if the science community got together and talked about how hated spiders can be and decided that if it had a moniker no one could pronounce, people would be less afraid of them. Somewhere along the way, however, the more general name *arachnid* was applied to the spider. My guess is that it was coined by a little lady named Muffet, who decided the spider needed a name that carried more weight on the fright side of the scale.

While *araneae* and *arachnid* are okay titles for spiders that crawl on trees or across the ground, I have my own pseudo-scientific name for the little intruders when they are suddenly caught crawling across my clothes. I call them *iiiyeee getoffme*.

More times than I care to remember the cursed little creatures are discovered on my person. I don't hesitate for one single second to abandon my self-imposed policy about sitting still in a deer stand. Without giving it one millisecond of extra thought, I go into self-defense mode. With a startled grunt and the fast flying flick of a finger, the intruder will either find itself airborne or, more likely, crushed flat by the gloved hand of human hatred.

As much as I dislike spiders, I've managed to glean some redeemable insights from them that I've written about in other books. For example, in my *Look at Life from a Deer Stand Devotional*, I highlighted two characteristics of spiders that are noteworthy. One is that its tiny size gives it an advantage not available to larger creatures. Because of its smallness, it can take up residence even in a palace and enjoy the food of kings. "What an inspiring picture this can be of how insignificance can be an advantage if used wisely. For example, think of how many employees who started as backroom janitor types that fed on the knowledge of a company's operation and ended up either owning that business or creating an improved version of it."[1]

Another interesting-yet-thought-provoking characteristic of the spider is its web. As amazingly intricate and beautiful as a fully woven web can be, the micro-thin, sticky strands that are used to make it have a rather sinister purpose. They are designed to trap other bugs so the spider can kill them and eat them (or save them for a later feast).

Though a web is an extremely effective weapon for the spider, I'm personally glad that the types found in Tennessee can capture nothing much larger than a fly. It was this limitation of the spider's web that led me down the path of imagination one morning while deer hunting. As I watched yet another spider build its trap, I quietly asked, "What if humans really were able to weave a web like the Spiderman character does?"

When the question crossed my mind I whispered to myself, "Now I know who got the idea for the Spiderman character. It had to be a hunter 'cause only people like us have enough time to sit and think of insane ideas like this!"

I proceeded to visualize a hunter in skintight camo instead of the red outfit that Spiderman wears. The hunter's superpowers gave him the ability to build a web big and strong enough across a deer trail to capture a trophy buck that was leaving a field and walking into a thicket. Then I went completely off the deep end and jumped to spring turkey season. I imagined a mature gobbler hanging in a web, flopping around trying to free itself.

I spent more time than I should have thinking about some of the other advantages that being able to weave a web would be for a hunter. Thoughts like how much cash we would save by not having to buy guns, bullets, and bows and arrows. Trespassers and poachers who came onto private land that we owned or leased could be dealt with very quietly…except for their screaming. We could go to the woods early in the morning, make a web, go home and watch a golf tournament or a football game on TV, and then go back that evening to gather up the meat. What a deal!

As wild as the thought of humans being able to weave webs might be, the truth is that we really can and do. How do I know? I've seen it done! Though the strands aren't actually tacky, clear strands like the fictitious Spiderman creates, they are just as real and a lot stickier than we expect. And the webs are extremely effective—but not in trapping food from the animal or insect kingdom. Instead, the web I'm referring to is the kind that traps the hearts and lives of humans. Here's a song lyric that explains one situation I witnessed.

The Tangled Web

Quiet room
Late night
Spend some time searching that site
Unaware that they're being led
Into a tangled web

Picture book
Familiar face
From another time and another place
Send the words—they might be read
It's a tangled web

New sparks from a flame that's old
Warm feelings where love has gone cold
Every line in the message makes another thread
To catch a heart
It's a tangled web

Quick reply,
"How do you do…"
"You're looking good."
"So are you!"
"It's been too long can we connect?"
It's a tangled web

Make up a reason
To take a trip
Secret place and a hello kiss
Stealing love
From someone else's bed
It's a tangled web

New sparks from a flame that's old
Warm feelings where love has gone cold
Every line in the message makes another thread
To catch a heart
It's a tangled web

Now what they do
Leaves them blind
Can't see the broken hearts left behind
Someday there's gonna be regrets
It's a tangled web [2]

This lyrical account unfortunately reflects a very real situation. Annie and I were quite shocked when we heard that a friend, I'll call her Joyce, had used social media to connect with an old boyfriend from high school who lived far away. After a few weeks of communicating via the Internet, she drove many hours to meet her former beau halfway between their two towns. A couple of months later she announced to her husband of nearly 40 years that she was leaving him to be with her old flame. At the same time, the man on the other end of the cyber connection broke the news to his wife that he was leaving her for his high school sweetheart.

When Joyce sent her first message to her old friend, it was probably innocent curiosity. His reply could have been equally harmless. However, at some point, perhaps at the second, third, or fourth exchange, something happened that turned their innocuous online visits into a desire to get together and kindle a forbidden romance.

On the surface, Joyce and her husband seemed to be getting along just fine. There was no hint of unhappiness or dissatisfaction with each other, and Joyce gave no signs of unrest in her marriage. Of course, we don't know what went on behind their closed doors.

Whatever the reason was for Joyce's decision to leave her husband and family, Annie and I are sure of a valuable lesson. When people allow themselves to entertain wayward thoughts, those thoughts can weave a mighty sticky and powerfully effective trap for them and others.

To guard our own marriage and help others, Annie and I discussed what Joyce could have done to avoid such a disastrous outcome. Naturally, the first thing we thought of was how dangerous the Internet can be. We know that the worldwide web is a very useful tool that can serve humanity in a very positive way, but in this case it served as a dark dungeon where a web of destruction was woven. Joyce could have immediately "unfriended" her old flame the moment she felt an errant emotion about him or he sent a message that suggested anything questionable. Of course, the man could have done the same thing.

Because the world of social media technology has inherent dangers, I urge all users—men and women—to make it a matter of utmost importance to be on guard against the threads of verbiage that are covered with the lethal glue of lust or potential attraction. As you connect with friends from the past or present, don't forget these lines in the lyric: "Every line in the message makes another thread to catch a heart...it's a tangled web." May those words echo in your head and in your heart the moment you detect something illicit in a message, whether it was sent to you or you thought of it.

There are other things you can do if the temptation comes to continue connecting with someone on the web who shows a questionable interest in you. A friend of ours did these things when an online exchange with an old friend heated up. He simply broke it off with the person, pulled out of that particular website's world, and changed his email address. And he never again checked the other person's site. His decision to disconnect from the website was a choice to keep his relationship with his wife and children strong. He has never regretted getting "off that grid" of the web.

Avoiding the specific social media website where the encounter took place and changing email addresses are commonsense suggestions. The problem is that common sense is hard to come by these days. It is nothing less than mind boggling to know that people who appear so sensible one day can be so insanely obsessed with the fantasy of forbidden love the next. But it happens because the spider of temptation weaves such masterful traps.

If you're a hunter and spend time in the woods, sooner or later you're going to see an *araneae* at work. When you do, it's okay to admire its amazing weaving skills. It still astounds me. But when you see the web, let it remind you to be careful when you're on the Internet. Your spiritual, emotional, and even physical life depend on your willingness to not get caught in the web of temptation.

> *He who dwells in the shelter of the Most High will abide in the shadow of the Almighty. I will say to the LORD, "My refuge and my fortress, My God, in whom I trust!" For it is He who delivers you from the snare of the trapper and from the deadly pestilence* (Psalm 91:1-3).

6

A Mutual Obsession

At the end of the ramp leading onto the interstate, I quickly glanced over my left shoulder and saw that it was safe to merge into the right lane. Several cars passed me on the left, barreling by well above the speed limit. As I accelerated to join the speeding masses a tall, heavy-built pickup truck roared by me on the left. The appearance of the truck made it very obvious that the owner wanted to be identified as a hunter. The custom paint job on the body was a full camo pattern, and the back window had white stickers in the shape of the animals that were likely the driver's preferred choices for chasing. On the left portion of the glass was a buck's head with antler tines that numbered well into the double digits. On the right was the outline of a six-by-six bugling bull elk. In the middle was a mature turkey gobbler in full strut.

As if the camo paint job and the window peppered with critter-shaped decals weren't enough to convince everyone on the highway how serious the owner of the truck was about hunting, there was a bumper sticker that put an exclamation point on the rolling statement. It read: "Hunting...It's Not Just a Passion, It's an Obsession!"

Because the truck was a rather blatant statement about the owner's apparent enthusiasm for his interest, and because there are plenty of folks who don't care for hunting and the people who do it, I imagined that some of the comments that were spoken in the privacy of some of the vehicles around us were less than favorable. They might have included:

- "Sick!"
- "Poor animals."
- "Pity *that* wife…"
- "Nut job!"
- "That's whacked."
- "Really?"

When it came my turn to do verbal commentary on the sight of the camo-covered pickup, I didn't say a single word for a few seconds. All I could do was smile. After surveying the paint job that was nothing short of a work of art, scanning the rear-window stickers, and processing the confession that was on the bumper, I finally sighed and said out loud, "All right! A man after my own heart!"

It wasn't easy to keep my eyes totally on the road as the truck shot by me. Besides its substantial height and length, I couldn't help but admire the huge knobby tires that were made for four-wheel, off-road driving. Though my window was up, I could hear the deep, manly voice of the tires as they sang across the pavement.

In harmony with the tires, I heard the perfectly timed clatter of the mighty diesel engine. Its commanding roar made my gas-powered truck motor whimper in fear, I'm sure. I totally enjoyed every second that I got to be next to my comrade in camo.

As if the driver could hear me, I spoke to the stranger in the big truck: "You can't tell by looking at my regular ole pickup that I'm one of you, my friend, but I imagine we could swap a few good stories. And if you knew where I was headin' right now, you'd want to fall in behind me and follow me there!"

My destination was a place about 40 miles west of the city of Nashville. It was a farm I often hunted that had lots of deer on the property and always held a ton of promise for sightings and success.

When I reached the place where the interstate forked, the truck peeled off to the left and headed toward downtown. I took the right turn that led away from the city and to the farm. I surmised that the hefty vehicle and its driver were on their way to spend the day surrounded by people and concrete instead of critters and timber. Assuming I was right, I felt sorrow for them, tipped my hat goodbye, and proceeded west out of town.

Though I assumed I would never meet the person in the well-designed truck, it was amazing how bonded I felt to whomever it was. While our rides were worlds apart in size and ornamentation, we were probably as close as brothers in mindset. In fact, I was sure we had at least three things in common when it came to hunting.

Wherever the critters are, that's where hunters want to go. Whether deer, turkey, elk, bear, rabbit, or any other animal, we want to know where they live and why they live there. Is it the acorns that keep their interest? The planted crops? The hiding places? The water source? One way or another, we'll find out what holds a particular animal to a piece of property, and that's where we'll be when hunting season starts.

In our area of the country, for example, every deer hunter knows that a prime spot to be during early bow season is near a persimmon tree. When I scout a new piece of property for hunting, finding a persimmon tree is like finding gold. Deer seem to enjoy persimmons like children enjoy ice cream.

Also while scouting, I do as much sitting and watching as walking around. Being at a field edge early in the morning or late in the evening can provide a huge payoff when it comes to knowing where the deer like to go. If I watch them come out of the woods and into a field consistently at a certain place, I consider it some major education about the whereabouts of deer. And keeping what I've learned in mind when hunting season starts will yield dividends in the form of venison. Such was the case on a particular farm here in Tennessee.

After watching and learning where the deer liked to go on the Webb place, I noticed they seemed to frequent an entrance into a field on the north end. Armed with that information and a compound bow, I took my portable stand to that spot and climbed into a tree on the first evening of the new season. Sure enough, about 30 minutes before dark a small herd of deer came through the woods heading right by me toward the field. Soon there was one less arrow in my quiver. It found its mark, and I felt satisfied that the time I'd taken to learn where the deer come and go had paid off.

By going often to where the deer go and storing away the knowledge gained from each time out, experience yielded benefits. But, liking to go where the animals go is not the only thing we hunters enjoy.

Hunters like to listen to what animals say, and we like teaching ourselves how to talk like them. For me, one of the most challenging sounds to imitate is the wild turkey. When I chase gobblers, I usually carry a bag full of tricks that help me sound like the girls and the boys. I can't say that I use them all that skillfully, but I enjoy working on the sounds and using them. While there are commercially produced recordings of all kinds that contain the yelps, clucks, and purrs that turkeys voice, nothing can tutor a hunter like the real thing in the wild. Sitting at daylight at the edge of a field next to a patch of woods where turkeys are known to roost is the best classroom any turkey hunter can attend. It's there that we can listen closely and learn how to say what they say and when to say it.

For example, as dawn approaches and the turkeys start to wake, we learn that they're not noisy risers. They usually begin with a light, prefly yelp. As the light gets brighter, the sounds turkeys make get a little louder. Eventually, if there are several birds roosted in the area, hunters will hear a choir of female yelps, clucks, and finally a "fly down" cackle accompanied by the distinct sound of flapping wings. Along with the "singing" hens, the rumble of mature gobblers thunders through the woods.

To a hunter's ears, hearing real turkeys talk is not just music—it's also valuable instruction. Each time I'm privileged to sit within earshot of a flock of birds as they talk their way through the morning wakeup and fly-down rituals, I listen attentively to each sound and try to memorize the tone and timing. When the concert is over, I know I'm one stroke of my box or slate call closer to perfecting my imitation of their language.

One of my favorite memories of being a "follower of the feather" and using some of the tutoring that the real birds offered was during a hunt only five minutes from my house. Turkey season was about half finished, and the birds had been hunted enough that they were extra skittish. For that reason, I went to the woods and field well before daylight so I wouldn't be easily seen when I walked to the spot where I wanted to set up.

With my shotgun loaded and laying across my lap and my calls on the ground next to me, sunrise slowly came. Up the field about 70 yards to my right I heard the first soft yelp. Fifteen seconds later I heard it again. Then another hen joined in. A third hen deeper into the woods behind those two lightly announced that she was awake. And then it happened. About 50 yards down the field edge, a male let go a gobble that made my hair stand on end. With the morning so calm, the volume of the gobbler's voice was almost shocking.

I worried that the boisterous gobble had made me flinch badly or caused me to yelp and give away my position. But when the first gobble was followed by another less than a half minute later, I braced myself for it and, at the same time, slowly reached for my push/pull box call. Confident that I'd gotten to the tree I was sitting against without being seen that morning, I decided to join in the morning song of the wild turkey. My hope was to convince the gobbler that a lone hen was to his left.

I carefully raised my legs so I could rest my shotgun on my right knee. Then I "voiced" a couple of soft yelps with the call. After I did, the tom yelled back. It was as though he were screaming, "Goodie, goodie, goodie!"

About three or four minutes passed, and the area grew a little quiet. That's when I enlisted what I'd learned from listening to turkeys on other mornings. I took off my baseball-type camo cap and held it by the bill in my right hand. With my left I pushed the little wooden rod of the box call and made the sound of a hen that sounded a little excited. I immediately followed the call with some wild flapping of my cap to make it sound like the wings of a hen flying to the ground. My intention was to make the gobbler think he'd heard the first of the girls flap their way to the ground.

I'd hardly laid the box call next to me and got my gun ready when the whooshing sound of soaring wings caught my ears. I tried not to let my eyes widen too much at the sight of what happened next. The gobbler that had responded to my calling flew down and landed within 12 yards of where I sat! He seemed quite surprised that there wasn't a hen in the immediate area. He looked around nervously. Before he had a chance to make a choice of whether or not to stay, my gun delivered a fatal load of buckshot to his brilliant-white head. The sun had barely peeked over the eastern horizon and my hunt was over—except for the cleaning and consuming.

Going where the critters go and learning how to say what they say are only two of the things I have in common with my unknown friend in the big hunter's truck.

The third thing hunters enjoy is learning what animals do and why they do it. Doing so yields an advantage for us that is very valuable. We start to think like the animal. This "oneness of mind" with the critters comes with time and experience. For example, I arrowed a sizable seven-point buck on a Tennessee farm. While tracking it, the blood trail led into a thicket. I decided to wait an hour before going in to give the deer time to expire. When I did enter the thicket, the blood trail stopped about 30 yards inside. I marked the spot with some white tissue, backed out, and waited some more.

Thirty minutes later I headed back into the thicket, and from the point of the last drop of blood I'd found, I stepped forward. Slowly and quietly I continued, all the while looking ahead of me as far as I could see into the dense foliage for visual signs of either a bedded or deceased deer. After about a minute or so of being intently engaged in searching for a body, I remembered to stop for a moment to look around my feet for more blood. When I did, I discovered that I was on a trail that was made and used by deer and other critters in the area. As though my mind was on the same page as the deer that lived on the farm, I was walking precisely where they walked.

Because I've followed enough deer through the tracking process, I was well aware that they will often stay on a familiar trail as they pass through a thicket, especially when wounded. After another two minutes of carefully following the trail, I found a pool of blood. It looked as though the deer had bedded and bled for a little while, gained some strength, got up, and moved ahead. But he didn't go far. Within another 25 yards I looked ahead and saw the buck lying lifeless beside the trail.

I suppose the owner of the huge, camo-clad truck will never know it, but I enjoyed the momentary companionship I felt with him on the interstate that day. Knowing that I wasn't alone in the enjoyment of going where the animals go, saying what they say, and doing what they do was a good feeling. And I'm under the impression that as obvious as the person had made it that hunting was his (or her) "thing," I suspect that like me it is a passion he will enjoy for as long as he lives.

There's one other thought about my encounter with the big truck and its owner that is worth mentioning. The three things I have in common with that person are very similar to what I desire as a follower of Christ. The root of this longing is found in John 5:19: "Jesus answered and was saying to them, 'Truly, truly, I say to you, the Son can do nothing of Himself, unless it is something He sees the Father doing; for whatever the Father does, these things the Son also does in like manner.'"

One of my greatest hopes is that I will successfully and victoriously follow Christ throughout all my days and follow Him into eternity. I know to do so I have to go where I see Him go, say what I hear Him say, and do what I see Him do. And the best place I can learn all of these is in His written Word.

For example, in the "going where Jesus goes" category, I think of the information related in Mark 1:35. Jesus gets up very early in the morning, while it was still dark, and goes to a secluded place to pray. If that is something He felt was important to do, then I know I too should follow His lead and escape from time to time into prayer. As a hunter, I especially like the part about getting up before dark and going to a quiet place.

As for saying what Jesus says, one example that I immediately think of is found in the story about the woman who was caught in the act of adultery. After challenging her accusers with His well-known words, "He who is without sin among you, let him be the first to throw a stone at her," the accusers gradually went away (John 8:7). There was no one left to stone the woman. Then Jesus offered the woman His tender compassion by saying to her, "I do not condemn you, either. Go. From now on sin no more" (verse 14). If Jesus is that compassionate with His words when it comes to sinners, then I need and want to follow His example.

When it comes to doing what I see Jesus do, I think of what He did when He heard that His friend Lazarus had died. John 11:35 simply records, "Jesus wept." Seeing in the Scriptures that my mighty Savior was moved to tears by the loss of His friend is my cue that it's okay to show emotion. To think that the One who was there when the universe was made, the One who endured the torture of the cross, and the One who defeated Satan and his hordes wasn't afraid to cry tells me that as a man I'm allowed to openly reveal the deepest feelings of my soul.

These are just a few biblical examples of how Christ is worthy to be followed and emulated. I joyfully admit that I want to do so with a zeal that is even greater than my passion for hunting—and that's a lot! I just hope that the guy or gal in the big hunter's truck feels the same way. If so, we're even more alike than I imagined.

Faithfully Follow You

Until I take my last step
Until I breathe my last breath
Until I close my eyes in death
I want to follow You

Until my race on earth is run
Until my work down here is done
Until the setting of my sun
I want to follow You

I want to go where I see You go
I want to say what I hear You say
I want to do what I see You do
I want to follow You
Faithfully follow You

And when it's time for me to cross that river
I want to follow You into forever[1]

7

Bullets and Believers

There are some very innovative products created for hunters that have made it on my "must have" list. Two of my favorites are:

- *Body warmers.* For hunting in frigid weather, I like the little, self-adhesive body warmers that heat up simply by opening the package. I buy them by the bagful and stick them on the bottom of my socks to keep my toes toasty. I found that if I also put them on each side of my back near the belt line, on my shoulders near my neck, and in the pockets that are integrated into my fancy balaclava in the area of my ears, I can stay on the stand much longer during the dead of winter.

- *Turkey straps.* For turkey hunting, my buddy Lindsey picked up an item for me that is very handy when I carry a big bird back to my vehicle. It's a two-inch wide strip of sturdy material and is very similar to a strap attached to a shoulder bag. One end is designed to loop around the turkey's head, and the other end splits and attaches around each foot. When properly attached, the combination of the strap and bird resembles a piece of luggage I would carry onto an airplane when traveling by air. It makes toting a big gobbler out of the woods so much easier. As a bonus feature, the shoulder pad that's included with the strap is blaze orange. It's a feature

that helps with safety since orange isn't required attire during Tennessee's spring gobbler season.

Not only do I like using items like the two just mentioned, I thoroughly enjoy going to our local big box hunting gear store and shopping for them. I candidly confess that if I exercised no financial restraint
whatsoever when I'm in the store, my cart would be piled high with
stuff. And the building behind my house where I keep all of my hunting gear would be bulging…more than it already is.

Knowing my propensity for overspending on hunting gear, I work
hard at controlling the amount of cash outlay I allow and use for it, but
it's not easy. One solution I've found that helps me manage the urge to
buy is to go to the hunting stores to *browse without buying*. In the same
way that my wife calms her appetite for chocolate by smelling it, I've
found that I can appease my urge for getting innovative equipment by
strolling through the store aisles and just looking at it.

One of the times I went into my favorite local outdoor outlet to do
a therapeutic, non-purchasing walk-through, I first spent some time
in the archery department and then moved to the treestand section. I
had no idea that when I wandered over to the bullet aisle I would find
something of great value. I discovered a very interesting and inspiring
connection between gun hunters and churchgoers.

With gun season only a few weeks away, I thought it would be good
to find out what cartridges were available for my .270 Ruger. Along
with several other shoppers, I stood in front of a 25-foot-long, multi-
tiered shelf that was nearly six feet tall. I studied the various velocity rat-
ings and bullet weights. I could hardly believe how many choices were
offered. The same was true for many other calibers. Even though the
national supply of ammo at the time was reputed to be below the normal level, this store's shelves were filled with box after box of bullets.

I noticed that some bullets came in full metal jackets, others had
expanding lead tips, some had hollow point, while others had plastic
ballistic tips. Some types had partitioned cores. There were cartridges
of silver while others were brass. The choices seemed endless.

As I stood there awestruck at the huge assortment, a fellow walked up and, without hesitating, took two boxes of 150-grain, soft-point, .270 shells off the rack. Less than a minute later, another guy stepped up and grabbed four boxes of .270 bullets that were 130 grain in weight. Watching all the ammo flying off the shelves made me feel a little concerned that if I waited too long to get my supply of bullets for gun season, I would miss my chance. So I went ahead and broke my "no buy" policy. I grabbed a couple of boxes of 150-grain, .270 cartridges, but I didn't leave the aisle. Instead, I lingered and simply watched the stream of bullet buyers as they came to the shelves.

Some of them stepped up and carefully read the information printed on the ends of the boxes before making a choice. Others came down the aisle, went straight to their preferred brand and caliber, took some boxes, and headed to the check-out counter.

It was clear to see that people had many different preferences when it came to ammo. In the five minutes or so that I observed the buying frenzy, I saw .308s, .243s, .30-06s, 7mm, .30-30 shells, and a few other calibers go into shopping carts.

I imagined how many answers I would have gotten if I'd asked some of the buyers why they chose the brand and type of bullets they took off the shelves. I probably would have heard everything from "These have worked for me since I was a teenager...no need to make a change now" to "My dad sent me for these, and he won't use any other brand. He told me if I came home with anything else he'd shoot me with them!"

I thought it was interesting to note that what one buyer liked in terms of bullet brand and caliber wasn't usually what the next guy preferred. The diversity of preferences was easy to see. Yet all the hunters who had come to get their ammo had a common goal in mind when it came to what they planned to do with it once they paid and left. Everyone would be aiming at bringing home wild game.

As I stood there that day, it occurred to me that those of us who go to Christian churches are not much different than hunters who go to buy bullets. We too have many preferences, yet we have one common goal. While we may think differently in areas such as worship style, taking of communion, dress codes, types of baptism, and outreach methods, our collective target is glorifying and honoring God.

The first time I noticed that not all Christians worshipped like I did was during my early teens. I grew up going to a church where our mode of worship was lively, enthusiastic, and audibly unreserved. We were a group that didn't hesitate to clap our hands and tap our toes with the music. Sometimes we dared to dance a little in response to the joy of knowing the Lord. We even washed one another's feet from time to time. These expressions of our faith were common for us, and I naively made the assumption that every church in town shared them. However, I eventually discovered that wasn't the case. It happened when a friend from school went to church with me.

Benny's parents were members of a congregation in our town that worshipped quite differently than we did. They enjoyed the structure of liturgy instead of the "free style" sharing my family and I were used to. They sang a lot of ancient hymns, and their accompaniment was a huge pipe organ. At our church the stage area was filled with guitars, a piano, percussion instruments of various kinds, and a tambourine or two. Sometimes even a banjo was added to the mix as we sang the current gospel songs that were popular. Their minister wore a robe and calmly stood in one place when he delivered his sermon. Our preacher wore a suit and would raise his voice as he walked from one end of the pulpit area to the other, sometimes even making it down the center aisle.

When our seven o'clock Sunday evening service kicked off with a rousing piano and guitar intro to the song "I'll Fly Away," Benny's body stiffened in shock. He looked at me wide-eyed and nervous as people jumped to their feet and joined in with hand clapping and energetic singing. I thought for a moment that my stunned friend might run from the building. After a few bars of the song had passed, a big smile came to his face. I realized he wasn't overly frightened by the worship. He was actually very intrigued by what he was seeing and hearing.

After the service ended, Benny admitted that when the music first started he thought, *Oh no! What have I gotten myself into?* His reaction was humorous, and our family still chuckles when we recall him saying to us, "I've had enough church tonight that I won't have to go again for a year!"

By going with me to church, Benny discovered there are other forms of worship besides the liturgical style. When I went with him to his home church, I learned that not every church was as lively as ours. I was amazed to learn, for example, that people could be quiet and joyous at the same time. As a result of visiting each other's pews, both of us were introduced to the fact that even though we were from very different church backgrounds, we could still be friends.

Basically, what Benny and I did was allow each other to be Christians despite our differences. To do otherwise would have promoted division, likely damaged our friendship, and definitely would have accomplished nothing toward unity in the Holy Spirit.

To illustrate how divisive it can be to expect everyone to worship exactly the way I do, imagine me standing in the bullet aisle at the big box hunting store. I'm at the .270-caliber section. Let's say that I'm there with the unwavering opinion that the .270 rifle is the one and only gun that is best for fulfilling the hunters' common goal of taking a deer.

Now suppose a fellow walked up beside me and reached for a box of 7mm shells. I slap his hand and say, "Hey, wrong bullet, buddy! You need to leave that 7mm behind and use a .270 like I do. If you don't, you're not really a hunter!" Then let's say that I promptly took the box of bullets out of his hand and put them back on the shelf. Can you fathom what might happen? I certainly can!

After my nose stopped bleeding, I would hope that getting my lights put out would help me see an important ray of truth. To tell a man that he's not a hunter because he doesn't use the size and brand of ammo that I use would not promote "unity in the community." In the same way, it would not be a good thing to discount someone's faith because he or she chooses to go to a different church than I do.

Unfortunately, in times past I've known some people who have considered it their duty to sow discord among believers by denouncing a denomination and the people in it. Divisive individuals like these are still around today, and they could learn a great deal from the hunters who were in the bullet aisle I was in. They would discover that the camaraderie between hunters who use guns is not based on what caliber we prefer or the brand of rifle we use to put the ammo in. Instead, our fellowship is rooted in the simple fact that we have a mutual interest in hunting.

In the world of hunters, I don't see the ".270 Church" criticizing the ".308 Church." I don't see the "Rifle Group" lambasting the "Pistol Packers." We're content to allow each other the freedom to carry whatever weapon we prefer to the woods. In a way, our acceptance of each other resembles how Benny and I let each other be Christians even though we didn't attend the same church.

Though we weren't consciously doing the right thing, my friend and I were displaying the kind of unity the apostle Paul was encouraging when he wrote to the church in Corinth about the issue. Apparently there were believers who were engaged in some serious conflict over their differences. They'd forgotten where true harmony was found. To address the division, Paul wrote:

> Now I exhort you, brethren, by the name of our Lord Jesus Christ, that you all agree and that there be no divisions among you, but that you be made complete in the same mind and in the same judgment. For I have been informed concerning you, my brethren, by Chloe's people, that there are quarrels among you. Now I mean this, that each of you is saying, "I am of Paul," and, "I of Apollos," and "I of Cephas," and "I of Christ." Has Christ been divided? Paul was not crucified for you, was he? Or were you baptized in the name of Paul?…Christ did not send me to baptize, but to preach the gospel (1 Corinthians 1:10-13,17).

Note that in his letter Paul clearly pointed to *Christ* as the central figure in the list of those people the Corinthians were saying they were following. It is obvious that Paul was pleading for them to remember that if they wished to be unified, Christ alone would need to be the focus of their fellowship.

Paul's plea that there be no divisions among God's people echoes the prayer of Jesus when He said "that they may all be one" (John 17:20). How exciting to think that Christ prayed about the unity of

His followers! It's thrilling because we can count on the prayers of Jesus being answered. We can look forward to the day when the redeemed (those who believe Christ alone is their only source of salvation) from all the ages will gather around the throne of God and there we will be one forever. Our eyes will be on Christ only instead of on the signs that sit by the road in front of our church buildings.

I'm well aware that just like there are bullets that aren't safe to use because of problems (such as insufficient powder or defective primers), there are church groups that are unsafe to attend because their teachings are biblically unsound. We all agree that our goal toward and promotion of righteousness would be benefited if these groups were culled. But for the most part, each Bible-based denomination has something redeemable to offer to the cause of the kingdom of God.

Think of church buildings like boxes of bullets on the shelves at the store. They come in many calibers, and the bullets inside are highly effective. May God give us all who are redeemed by His grace an extra measure of compassion so that we will be gracious to one another as we seek to glorify and honor Him. After all, every "blood bought" bullet in every Bible-based church box is headed to the same target.

One in Christ
Blood-washed pilgrims on the highway
Chant the sweet, melodious strain
Of their freedom from confusion,
Angels join the glad refrain;
One with all the hosts of heaven,
There their names are written down;
Jesus only, Jesus ever,
In their hearts as King they crown. [1]

8

He Cares

Billy's cell phone buzzed in the middle of a lunch meeting with his fellow production managers at the furniture factory where he worked. As he kept talking, he pulled the phone out of his shirt pocket to see whose name was in the window. It was his wife calling from their home.

"Sorry, guys. I gotta take this call." He left the table and clicked the answer button. "Hey, babe. What's up?"

Cindy's voice sounded a little strained. "Your mom called, and she's worried about your dad."

Billy heard his wife's worry in her voice. "What's up with Dad? Everything okay?"

"Well, your dad went hunting this morning and promised he'd be back home before 11 o'clock, but he's not back yet."

Billy felt a wave of relief. He tried to pass the reassurance on to his wife. "Dad's probably involved in tracking a wounded deer. We hunters can get so focused on a blood trail that we forget important stuff like calling and letting people know what's going on."

Cindy didn't want to counter with what she had to say next, but she did so as calmly as she could. She knew it would likely prompt her husband to drop what he was doing and go to the farm where his dad was hunting.

"Billy, your mom said your dad called her about 8:30 this morning from the woods and reported he wasn't feeling well. He told her he'd climbed out of his treestand, the one on the backside of the property, and was going to walk back to the truck and head home. She hasn't heard from him since. It's now past noon. That's why she's worried."

Billy couldn't speak for a few moments as he processed what he'd heard.

"That doesn't sound good. I think I'd better wrap up my meeting here and head to the farm. Call me if you hear from Mom, especially if she tells you Dad is home."

Cindy ended the call and said a prayer for her father-in-law. As she looked out of their kitchen window toward the east where her worried husband would be going, she said a prayer for him as well.

Billy went back to the lunch table and announced that the meeting would have to end and told them why. His friend Keith insisted on going along, and Billy took him up on the offer. With his imagination running wild with worry about what might have happened to his dad, Billy knew the 20-minute drive they were going to make would seem like 20 hours.

Keith held on as Billy sped around the turns that took them out of the factory property and onto the main highway. Once they reached the edge of town and less traffic, he hoped it might help to talk and distract his friend with some conversation.

"Tell me about your dad, Billy. How long has he been a hunter?"

It took a few seconds for Billy to answer, but he finally did.

"Dad's been a hunter since he was just a kid. My grandpa—his dad—introduced him to squirrel hunting at around six years old. When he was only eight, he got his first deer. That's mighty young to start hunting, but there weren't a ton of regulations regarding kids at that time. Hunting got into his blood. I don't know anyone who loves the challenge of a hunt more than my dad."

Keith noticed that it seemed to help his friend to talk, so he probed a little more.

"How old were you when your dad took you hunting for the first time?"

Billy half smiled. "Much to my mother's protests, Dad took me with him to a deer stand when I was four years old. I remember it as vividly right now as I ever did. I can still smell the coffee in the Thermos he opened while we were sitting in the old wooden treestand together. I wanted to take a drink, but he wouldn't let me. He had a little bottle of orange juice for me…and a Snickers bar. Dad tried to keep the news from Mom about what he gave me for breakfast, but leave it up to a kid to tell everything."

With five more miles to go on the main highway before turning onto the narrow gravel road that led to the farm, Keith kept the conversation going.

"Isn't your boy about four years old now?"

"Yes, he is. And I figure I can't break tradition. I plan to take him hunting with me this fall. I bought a pop-up blind just so BJ can move around when he wants to. Cindy's not crazy about the idea, but she understands. She voiced her worry, but she also believes it will be good for us to be in the woods together. My dad can't wait to be there the first time BJ goes. It'll be tight in the tent, but that's what family and hunting is all about—being tight."

The conversation ended when Billy turned onto the gravel road. White dust billowed behind his pickup as he hurried toward the blue metal gate where he'd park. Keith saw that his friend's expression had turned very serious as he pulled up along the fence next to his dad's pickup and turned the engine off. He pointed toward an opening in the distance between two patches of woods.

"We're going to walk across this field and go through that opening in the trees. The stand Dad went to this morning is a 10- or 12-minute walk beyond that point. As we go, keep scanning the area all around us…just in case."

A chill hit Keith from the way Billy paused before he said "just in case." Keith tried to lighten the moment.

"Sounds like your dad knows what he's doing out here. I suspect he's just fine."

"You're right. What I'm hoping is that you and I are going to be helping a 65-year-old hunter drag a monster deer back to the gate. But we'll head to the stand first to make sure he's not there."

Billy didn't take the time to unlock the gate and walk through it. Instead, he quickly climbed over it and Keith followed. Not wasting any time and moving at a fast pace, they topped the last rise before being at a place where the stand could be seen. Billy stopped and took out his cell phone. After touching the speed dial number for his dad, he put the phone on speaker. The two of them listened as his dad's phone rang several times through the speaker before going to voice mail.

"Hey, this is William. I'm probably hunting and can't answer. Leave a number, and I'll call you back."

Keith smiled. "He is a diehard hunter, isn't he?"

Billy didn't answer as he touched the off button on his phone. He started walking quickly as he put it back in his pocket. "Dad usually puts his phone on silent when he's hunting but it was worth a try."

Billy looked toward the hill where the treestand was located. He spotted the familiar platform made of treated lumber and saw that it was empty. He visually followed the 2 x 4 steps down the tree to the ground. Because of the camo clothing his dad was wearing, at first Billy missed the form of a man sitting at the base of the tree. Realizing something seemed odd, he kept looking. When he finally realized what he was seeing, his face turned pale.

"Dad!" Billy's yell reverberated powerfully through the woods. He didn't get an answer, and he yelled louder as he sped up his pace. "Dad!"

Still seeing no movement, he broke into a hard run. Keith fell in behind him, and the two of them jumped over and around the natural debris on the floor of the woods. After a fast descent into a ravine and an even faster climb up the other side, they made it to the flat where the treestand was located. Billy stopped when he got about 10 yards from his dad.

His rifle lying on the ground at his side, his father was sitting with his back against the tree. His head was bowed as if he were praying or sleeping.

Though William's hat covered most of his face, Keith could see enough of his skin to notice it was an eerie gray color. His soul ached when he glanced over at Billy and saw the look on his friend's face. Billy had noticed it too. Keith watched as the weeping son slowly covered the remaining yards and knelt in front of his dad.

Billy didn't touch him. Instead, he leaned down low enough to look up at his face. "Dad? Are you ok? Are you asleep?" he asked softly. "Can you hear me?" After waiting a few seconds, Billy put his hand on his dad's shoulder and gently shook it. There was no reaction from his dad.

Keith knelt next to Billy but didn't say a word. Both men's eyes were glistening with tears as they processed the reality they didn't want to face.

Finally Billy spoke. "I think he's gone, Keith. Dad's gone." After a pause, Billy cried out, "Oh, God, this can't be happening!"

Billy and Keith stood and then sat down on the dry leaves around the tree, Billy next to his dad. Billy kept hoping his dad would lift his head and say something, but it didn't happen. Keith dreaded to say what had to be said.

"Billy?" Keith kept his voice gentle. "We have to notify some folks about this. I say we call 911 and find out who needs to come out here to help."

"You're right, Keith. I know you're right. But let's give Dad a few more minutes. Maybe he'll come around."

Billy knew he was only delaying the inevitable, but he felt compelled to wait.

Keith put his arm around his friend and patted his shoulder. "Take as long as you want, Billy. If it's all right with you, I believe I can find my way back to the gate. I'll call for help and wait for the people there."

"Thanks, man. When they come to where we're parked, call me so I know you're coming. I'll be right here. Give me five minutes before you call anyone so I can call Mom and my wife."

When the sound of Keith's footsteps faded beyond the rise, Billy sat next to his dad and wept. The dread he had in his heart about calling his mother and Cindy was almost more than he could bear. Finally he gathered the nerve to do it, knowing it would be the worst call his mother could imagine.

He cried harder as he called his mom and broke the news. There

was another flood of tears when he spoke to Cindy. When he was through with the calls, he felt weary under the burden of sorrow. Weak and broken, he leaned against the tree his dad was leaning against. He was shoulder to shoulder with his father. Billy looked up at the afternoon sky that was deep-blue and felt hot tears run down his cheeks and jaw as he whispered toward the heavens. "God, how am I gonna get through this? How's Mom gonna get through it? What about my boy who loves his grandpa? What's he gonna do? And Cindy? Oh, God, please have mercy on us."

Billy didn't say another word or ask God another question for several minutes. He put his head back against the tree trunk. He couldn't look at his dad's lifeless body even with his peripheral vision without sobbing, so he kept his eyes closed and waited for Keith to return with help. He searched his mind for something that might ease the pain of despair.

Not being heavily into music, he never expected a song to come to mind at such a time and offer needed consolation. He was surprised when he remembered an old hymn that had given his dad great comfort when his only brother passed away. The two men had been very close. Billy remembered his dad playing the song over and over. He could almost hear his dad's voice as he sang along with the quartet. Though Billy's voice felt weak and shaky, he sang as much of the song as he could remember:

> Does Jesus care when I've said "goodbye"
> To the dearest on earth to me,
> And my sad heart aches, till it nearly breaks,
> Is it aught to Him? Does He see?
>
> Oh yes, He cares, I know He cares,
> His heart is touched with my grief;
> When the days are weary, the long nights dreary,
> I know my Savior cares. [1]

Billy sang through the only verse he could remember and the chorus a few times. Each time the river of tears grew deeper, yet the pain of sorrow seemed to ease a bit. He knew the sting of finding his dad at the base of one of his favorite deer stands would likely never go away completely, but he also realized this melody was one he would hum when the waves of sorrow rose.

Billy's parents had made advance plans regarding what to do when one of them died. They'd agreed to be cremated, and each of them chose where their ashes were to be placed. The locations were included in the instructions in their wills. When Billy and his mother opened the envelope, they read William's last request: "Put my ashes at the base of the tree on the backside of our farm. Scatter them there and let them fertilize that mighty oak. I want it to stay strong so Billy and BJ can use the stand that's in it."

As instructed, William's ashes were scattered around the last tree he'd climbed and the one he'd designated as his final resting place. On the trunk of the tree is Billy's handiwork. Using his dad's favorite hunting knife, he carefully carved into the bark two words from the song that meant so much to his dad and now to him: "He cares."

Humble yourselves under the mighty hand of God...casting all your care upon Him, for He cares for you (1 Peter 5:7 NKJV).

9

Start Countin'

After ascending a tree with my portable stand to about 14 feet above the ground, I tethered my safety harness to the trunk and settled into the seat. The light of dawn began to chase away the darkness that had concealed my walk up to the ridge. For several days I'd looked forward to this morning hunt for Tennessee whitetail using my 50-caliber muzzleloader. The excitement I felt about what might happen in the next few hours helped lessen the sting of the deep chill in the air.

Thirty minutes passed, and some of the rays of the sun that filtered through the leafless trees blazed on my camo coat and provided two helpful benefits. The warmth that found its way inside my clothing gave me an extra measure of endurance against the unusually low, early November temperature that had fallen on our region. More importantly, the relief I felt from the cold helped me fend off one of the most annoying phenomena that winter hunting can cause—the shakes.

The only thing worse than the trembles that the cold can generate is the timing of them. It seems that the shakes only happen just prior to spotting an approaching deer. And it seems that whatever effect the icy air has on the muscles is cruelly doubled when buck fever grips the brain. Thankfully, that morning I didn't have to deal with the shot-hindering body quivering that the combination of cold muscles and red-hot buck fever can cause. I smiled in my comfort as I waited.

A full hour passed, and by then I was experiencing a perfect blend of chill and warmth. I unzipped my coat halfway so I could enjoy the mixture and continued to watch the ridge before me and behind me. That's when the morning got really interesting.

From somewhere behind the tree I was in I heard the familiar sound of the crunches that deer hooves make in dry leaves. I'd learned to distinguish them from the light rustle of leaves a squirrel or chipmunk can create. I was quite sure that something large was moving my way. And since we don't have bears in our neck of the woods and the farm I was hunting had no cattle on it, I was 99.99 percent positive I needed to prepare my gun for action.

Another couple of minutes passed, and curiosity got the best of me. I was unable to stop myself from shifting a little in my stand seat to see if I could look around the tree and get an eye on whatever was coming in. As I turned, the aluminum frame of my climber did me no favor when it creaked. At the same instant, I saw the critter that had made the noise in the leaves.

I usually don't number the points on a buck if it looks sizable. In our state, a rack that is wide enough to extend beyond the ears is going to be a prize to take home no matter what the tally of tines might be. However, because the buck had heard the metallic pop of my stand frame when I moved, he was standing motionless about 30 yards away looking in my direction. That gave me time to note that he was a really nice nine pointer.

It was a good thing that the effects of the cold had completely passed, otherwise the jitters that I suddenly had to battle would have been worse than they were. I tried not to allow my head to bob with excitement as I strained to not move while watching the buck stare toward my tree. My neck started hurting during the lengthy standoff between us. The growing ache in my body started tampering with my mental faculties. I realized the fever I was feeling was starting to steal the confidence that I would need to close the deal on the deer I hoped would continue to approach.

What the deer didn't know was that this wasn't the first time I'd been at the challenging place where man and beast are in a war of wits. And on enough occasions I'd won the battle. I learned something from each one that helped me with the next. One of the things I brought from the previous hunts was a method for confidence building that involved counting.

The first time I used the counting tactic was with a West Virginia buck. I won't forget the feeling of despair that rushed in when the sight of him coming up a hillside toward my location completely erased my knowledge on what to do. I was so rattled by his appearance that I couldn't think straight. I had to look down at my .30-30 lever action to remember where the safety button was located. Knowing that my mind had turned to mush and if I didn't do something quick I was going to mentally lock up, I whispered silently, "Okay, Bubba, one, your gun really is loaded. Two, you've practiced shooting and you know the sights are right. Three, that buck doesn't know you're near, the wind is in your favor, and all is well. Four, relax, man, and move slow when it's time to move."

For some reason the self-coaching calmed my nerves enough that the knowledge necessary to raise my gun and take the shot returned to my frazzled brain. Since that day I've chuckled about how undone I was by the approaching deer and how I had to count facts to take him. But I'd discovered a technique that worked in my favor! And I've repeated it many times.

Now, back to that "large by Tennessee standards" nine-point buck that was staring at me. I found it necessary to do some counting. "One, he doesn't look excessively nervous about the noise my stand made. Two, there really is powder and bullet in my gun and a firing cap on the nipple. [I was so rattled that I couldn't remember if I'd loaded the muzzleloader!] Three, the breeze is in my favor. Four, everything's good... let him walk on in. You can do this!"

As it turned out, the buck did indeed relax and started slowly feeding toward me. I didn't move a muscle for fear that a joint in my stand—or my body—would creak. My eyes watered with excitement when he made a 90-degree turn approximately 15 yards from me and started walking toward the dirt road that ran through the woods.

When he reached the logging road he turned left again and meandered down it. Finally he was at an angle that didn't require me to shift around in the seat and risk the stand making noise again. All I had to do was twist my upper body a little, raise the rifle, take aim through the open sights, and fire. When I did, smoke bellowed out of the barrel and hid the world from view for a few seconds. When the cloud cleared and I could see through the woods once more, I saw the buck's white belly about 10 yards inside the woods on the other side of the dirt road. The deal was done! Once again the counting method served me well.

The deer woods is not the only place that the counting method is useful for restoring some needed confidence. During a particularly tough time in the life of our family, my wife, Annie, came up with a list of three absolutes that she started repeating whenever fear and doubt crept in to destroy the peace in her heart that was precious to her. She would say, "God loves me. He's in control. And I can trust Him." If necessary, she would take in a deep breath, exhale slowly, and repeat the list. The renewed assurance these truths generated in her mind and heart were visible on her face. She would put her shoulders back, stand tall, and go about her everyday business remarkably comforted. Then after a while, if thoughts of doubt returned to destroy and threatened to crumble her spirits, I would hear her say again, "God loves me. I can trust Him. He's in control!"

I was astonished and excited to see how transforming those three proclamations could be. And not just for Annie. I've added them to my arsenal of defense against unwelcomed despair. In one moment I can be fretting about a matter that could potentially yield a destructive result; in the next, after stating and sometimes restating the trio of truths about God's care, I can feel settled and confident that my world will not end. One example of how this counting tactic brought some needed comfort to me involved a health issue.

One day a headache came that wouldn't subside. For 10 days I was miserable. Traveling and performing concerts during those days made the pain even worse. About five days into it, a rash appeared on my back and legs. Finally, I could take no more and headed to an emergency room. When the nurse who took down my information saw the rash, I noticed her facial expression change to include shock. Her words that followed were, to say the least, disconcerting.

She sat up straight and said, "Oh my!"

Within seconds I was put on one of their rolling beds and taken to an isolation room. A doctor in a mask came in and asked questions, writing down what I assumed were my answers on his clipboard.

He could see that the headache had taken its toll. He said a few things that I don't remember and left the room. The next thing I knew I had a needle in my arm and a bag of morphine dripping into my veins. The relief that the drug gave from the hammer that had pounded at my brain for so long was instantaneous. I jokingly said to the nurse who attended me that I wanted a 50-gallon barrel of the stuff that was in the plastic bag…to go. She gave me a courtesy smile as if she'd never heard that request before.

When the doctor came back into my room a few minutes later, he sat down and pulled his wheeled throne up to my bedside. He lowered his mask and spoke with tenderness. He calmly "suggested" that a procedure be done that I'd never experienced. He wanted to do a spinal tap to check to see if I might have meningitis.

The words "spinal" and "tap" should never be used in the same sentence. The idea of combining a delicate spine with what maple syrup farmers do to a tree isn't one that soothes my soul. But the truth was I really had no choice.

Once again the doctor left the room.

I lay there in the quiet with my thoughts that were churning toward very real fears and frightening questions. Is it gonna hurt? What if they hit a nerve that does permanent damage? What if they find meningitis?

As a hunter, I talk about the trembles that come with buck fever as if it were a bad thing. In reality, I love 'em. Getting the shakes at the sight of an incoming monster buck is what keeps me going back to the woods. However, the trembling that came with the uncertainty I felt about the approaching monster of a long needle sliding into my back wasn't something remotely enjoyable. I felt a total lack of confidence that I was going to be able to successfully handle what was about to happen. And then I remembered the helpful method. "It's time to start counting!"

Under my breath as I watched the door for the arrival of the needle bearer, I whispered, "One, God loves me. Two, He's in control. Three, I can trust Him." I waited and watched and went through the list again.

"One, He loves me. Two, He's in control. Three, I can trust Him."

I'm not sure how many times I repeated those truths, but I'm sure they helped me follow the doctor's orders and not flinch as he did what he had to do. While I suppose I could credit the effects of the pain medicine to some degree, I believe the incredibly steady and skilled hands of the young doctor who inserted the needle into my spine, simple human endurance, and the bolstering of my confidence through the counting method that reminded me of God's care and control were the main factors in tolerating such an invasive procedure. I credit God's divine intervention for getting me through it successfully. I know that He really does love me enough to oversee my safety, that whatever the diagnosis, He is in control, and He can be trusted with the outcome.

With the hospital room empty again, it was time to wait for the results of the examination of the spinal fluid. I did plenty more counting during those two long hours. Finally the doctor reappeared and announced that the fluid was clear and showed no signs of meningitis. The relief that flooded my spirit was even better than the effects of the morphine!

Though he wasn't fully certain, the emergency room doctor decided that I'd likely experienced an inflammation of blood vessels, a condition known as vasculitis. I was instructed to visit a dermatologist and get a biopsy on one of the sites where the rash had appeared. Later I learned that if it were indeed vasculitis, it could have attacked my heart, my major organs, or my skin. If the heart or major organs had been targeted, it could have been life-threatening. In my case, with only my skin being affected, I was very fortunate. I thank God to this day that I'm still around.

As I often do when my life has been so deeply touched by a situation, I expressed my thoughts in a song. I hope the following lyric will help you remember the counting method that I've used so effectively in that hospital emergency room, on deer stands, and in other places. I'm sure it will help you too! The next time you're in a deer stand and an approaching monster buck unravels your nerves, you're welcome to start counting. In fact, I highly recommend it. Or if you find yourself facing a struggle in life outside the hunter's woods, I recommend encouraging yourself by numbering the facts about God's care for you. In either case, you'll find that it helps you regain much-needed confidence.

I'm Countin' on Him

I've been walkin' this narrow way
Long enough to know there's gonna be
    some days when
I find myself worryin' and doubtin'
And that's when I start countin'...

One...God loves me, this I know
Two...He's always in control
Three...I can trust Him...even when
I'm not sure where He's leadin' me
He's my dependable friend,
    and I'm countin' on Him

Now in those times when the road gets steep
Burdens slow me down...I just tell my feet, "Hey,
Don't stop now; keep movin' up this mountain!"
That's when I start countin'...

One...God loves me, this I know
Two...He's always in control
Three...I can trust Him...even when
I'm not sure where He's leadin' me
He's my dependable friend,
    and I'm countin' on Him

Oh, when troubles come like a flood
And they try to pull me under
I can raise my hand and tell that trouble
I'm livin' life by the numbers...oh...

One…God loves me, this I know
Two…He's always in control
Three…I can trust Him…even when
I'm not sure where He's leadin' me
He's my dependable friend,
and I'm countin' on the

One…who loves me this I know
Two…He's always in control
Three…I can trust Him…even when
I'm not sure where He's leadin' me
He's my dependable friend,
and I'm countin' on Him[1]

10

While You Were Away…

My old friend John lives three states away, so the opportunities to hunt with him have been far too few for the last several years. However, we've enjoyed swapping stories about our adventures. One of my favorites is about what happened to him and another buddy during a deer hunt many seasons ago. With his permission, this is my version of his story.

▷·⬦·○·⬦·◁

John and his friend Greg convinced their wives that if they were ever going to have the thrill of tagging a trophy "wall hanger," they would have to leave the rolling hills of their small farms and go hunt in the distant, tall mountains of their state. With their wives having caved to their pitiful pleas, the two friends planned a five-day journey into the mountains in one of the state forests to hunt whitetail.

John's wife, Bettie, said the two men were as excited as two little boys playing together as they prepared for their trip. The list of equipment they would take was nearly as long as the truck that would carry them to their destination. The pickup barely held all the gear they loaded. With the bed fully loaded and the tires straining to hold up the weight of all their stuff, the two men waved goodbye to their wives and headed northeast. The closer they got to the towering mountains,

the bigger the deer grew in their minds…and in their conversations as they talked about the hunt.

The first day was filled with mostly driving to their destination. Their mid-afternoon arrival allowed enough time to find a camping spot, secure the truck, grab their rifles, and head to the woods. Instead of actively hunting, they split up and spent the rest of daylight walking around the area scouting for a place that looked "deerish" enough to return to the following day.

When darkness fell, they met back at their campsite, settled in for the evening, and reported their findings. John's tree of choice overlooked a long flat about three-fourths of the way up the mountain where there were plenty of acorn-laden oaks. Greg's chosen spot was the edge of a small field on a high ridge.

About four o'clock the next morning, the minute hand of their wind-up clock pulled the trigger of the alarm. Like two bullets out of a .30-30, the pair shot out of their sleeping bags. Well in advance of the sun's first peek over the mountaintops, they were fed and dressed in camo. They laced their boots, shouldered their guns, and walked up the steep trail that would led them up the mountainside.

Before the two of them separated for the morning, they stood on the path and talked quietly about how grateful they were that it appeared as though there were no other hunters around. They knew it was one of the advantages of taking their vacation days to hunt during the week instead of going on Saturdays when all the weekend warriors spilled onto public land in search of whitetails.

Feeling relieved to be there alone, they offered their well wishes to each other and disappeared into the dark. It was a routine they would follow for the next four days.

Though they had a mountain-sized week of fun, Friday evening came with no shots fired. It was as though the deer knew the woods were empty so they could feed at night, lie down in the daytime, not move, and be safe.

As the two tired and disappointed hunters drove out of the remote, government-owned land on Friday evening and back toward civilization, they noticed the weekend warriors pouring onto the access roads.

The sight of a line of trucks and Jeeps passing by them in the opposite direction made them feel both good and bad. On one hand they would be out of the mountains before the crowd gathered. It was a matter of safety. Too many times through the years they'd heard about hunters getting shot in woods by unethical, untrained, and even inebriated deer hunters who would shoot at anything that moves and discover what it was after the fact.

On the other hand, as they watched the incoming parade of hunters heading toward where they'd been, John and Greg knew that the deer they'd not seen all week would be forced to be up and running because of the masses of people wandering the woods. As a result, the mountains they'd just left that had been silent would be filled with loud echoes of gunfire. It was hard to face the fact that someone among the weekend group of public-land hunters would find the deer that might have been theirs.

As they completed the 20-mile drive back to the nearest town from their campsite, the two hunters agreed that it would be prudent to call home and let their wives know they were on their way home to their waiting arms. Since they had no cell phones, they stopped at a gas station and made their calls. That's when John learned some news that wasn't easy for him to process. He didn't want to tell Greg about it either. However, he climbed back into the truck cab, started the motor, and let it idle as he spoke.

"You're not gonna believe this, Greg. And I'm not sure if I should even tell you because I'm not gonna live this down for the rest of my life."

Greg wasn't sure what his buddy was talking about, and he waited anxiously for at least 15 seconds before he prompted John. "Well, are you gonna tell me or not, man? You baited me good. I'm on the hook. Reel me in. What happened?"

John sighed deep, bit his lip, and then looked straight ahead as he talked. He didn't have the nerve to look at his friend while he gave him the news. "Bettie just told me she killed a huge nine-point whitetail off our back porch two days ago."

Greg looked at John for a few seconds and then turned and looked to his right, gazing out the passenger window. He couldn't bear the thought of his good buddy seeing him smile so big that his jaws were about to dislocate. He didn't say a word for several seconds as he regained his composure. Finally he offered his best fake attempt at consoling John. "Well, my friend, you and I both know that sometimes life just ain't fair. I know what you spent on this hunt 'cause I spent the same amount. I know how much energy you put into it too 'cause I'm just as tired as you are. I know you feel like fate just kicked you in the hiney, and man, I feel for you. It's just not…" Greg suddenly stopped talking and turned really quiet. After a few moments he readjusted his posture in the seat and then took his cap off and started rubbing his forehead with his free hand.

John knew his friend's gestures well enough to know that he was dealing with some disturbing thoughts. "What is it? What are you thinking, Greg?"

"Good grief, John. Do you reckon Bettie has told Nancy about the buck?"

All at once the full implication of his buddy's question dawned on John. He started laughing so hard he was afraid he'd hyperventilate. He struggled to answer Greg through his wails of laughter. "It might have been Bettie who tagged a big deer in our backyard while we were 200 miles away looking for one just like it. But it's not just me whose gonna have to face the music with family, friends, and our other huntin' friends." John pounded the steering wheel as he laughed some more. Then he continued. "Of course Nancy knows about the buck! By now she's probably told everybody she knows just like Bettie has. We're cooked, man. We are toast!"

Greg lowered his head and shook it from side to side. "John, there's only one thing we can do about this."

"What's that, good buddy?"

"We gotta drive to Canada 'cause we can't go home now!"

Though their egos were shattered by the ordeal they suffered when they got home, eventually John and Greg were able to laugh when others poked them in the ribs with their own story. And I'm among those who enjoy turning it on them occasionally. It also provided some good material for swapping tales with other hunters. I especially like to tell it to the married hunter who is planning a faraway trip to chase big game and who lives on farmland with a wife who knows how to handle a rifle. He deserves a fair warning about what could happen while he's away.

While John and Greg's experience has an element of humor, there's a sobering resemblance to another story I heard that has been around at least a hundred years. Though it originated over a century ago, the incredibly life-changing insight in it is as timely today as it was back then. I adapted the old story into this song lyric.

Acres of Diamonds

I heard about a farmer plowing in his dirt
Fighting sweat and blisters and all the rocks
　　that made it worse
Then one day a man came by and said,
"There's wealth out there in diamonds!"
He sold his farm and all he had,
And headed out to find 'em

He followed all the rumors and drifted town to town
There were diamonds in his dreams at night
But nothing in the ground
When he spent every dime he had
And his hopes were gone forever
They say he took his empty life
And drowned it in a river

But he didn't know all along
What they found on his old farm
While he searched the whole world over
For the wealth he never found
There were acres of diamonds
back at home in the ground

I can't help but wonder how many times
That same story has been written
In the hearts of other lives
Who just can't see that in their homes
Is all they ever wanted
Still they leave it all behind
and end up like the farmer

He didn't know all along
What they found on his old farm
While he searched the whole world over
For the wealth he never found
There were acres of diamonds
back at home in the ground [1]

Unlike John and Greg who were aware of the treasure that was found in their backyard while they were away, the farmer in the "Acres of Diamonds" story died not knowing what he'd left behind. What a sad ending to his life. Oh how different it could have been for him if he'd been able to go back home and enjoy the wealth that had been there all along. His story could have ended like the prodigal son's, whose experiences as a wanderer is recorded in God's Word.

The account of this young man who demanded his inheritance from his father and used it to feed his insatiable desire for pleasure is familiar to most of us. We read it and feel sad for him when we see how his wasteful spending led him to survive only by eating the food scraps that were fed to pigs. We are relieved when we get to the part that says, "But when he came to his senses, he said, 'How many of my father's hired men have more than enough bread, but I am dying here with hunger! I will get up and go to my father'" (Luke 15:17-18).

Upon his return to his home, the prodigal son learns there is nothing more valuable in the whole world than his father's love, which includes his tender forgiveness and unconditional acceptance. It is a timeless story that can inspire anyone who has lost hope because of a fruitless search for some type of elusive diamond.

On a spiritual level, the stories of John and Greg, the wandering farmer, and the prodigal son bring to mind a question that each of us needs to ask: "Is there anything outside of my relationship with God that appears to be bigger or better and tempts me to leave Him and go look for it?" Could it be wealth and the power and influence that go with it? Could it be the affection of another person or a longing to feel accepted in a certain social circle? Is it fame that entices?

Whether the temptation is any of these longings or another desire that would draw us away from the joy of a close relationship with Christ, may we never forget how foolish it would be to allow it to make us forget that in Jesus we already have everything we need to be happy, satisfied, and content. For that reason, I want to stay rooted in Jesus. How about you?

> *Blessed be the God and Father of our Lord Jesus Christ, who has blessed us with every spiritual blessing in the heavenly places in Christ* (Ephesians 1:3).

FULL DRAW

*Dedicated to the hunters who
willingly sacrifice their days in the field
for the sake of caring and providing for those they love.*

*Until another morning finds you in the hunter's woods,
may the reading of these pages somehow serve,
if only in a small way, to fill the gap.
May God honor your faithfulness.*

1

꘎꘎꘎꘎꘎

Nearly 20 minutes had passed since the buck appeared down the ridge. The big woods were clear enough, even with the early October foliage, that Joe Tanner was able to spot the rack the heavy whitetail sported. He had seen the huge animal a time or two during his scouting trips before archery season opened. The velvet was gone from the antlers, and the 10 points glistened in the morning sun. Joe was grateful for the encounter. His heart was about to explode with excitement as his left hand tightened on the grip of his compound bow.

The large number of white oak acorns that lay on the forest floor like candy on a plate caused the deer to slowly feed toward Joe's treestand. While the animal's appetite was being satisfied, Joe took the opportunity to begin rising to his feet, hoping that no creaks or snaps would result while shifting all of his weight onto the platform that towered 18 feet above the ground. Finally, mission accomplished, he stood motionless as the deer intermittently fed and raised his head to scan the woods for danger. The awesome creature did not suspect that the keeper of his fate was looming above him. The buck continued to feed, moving toward the hunter's pounding heart.

Joe was relieved to see that the old buck was alone. There were no other sets of eyes to detect his movements, no other witnesses to their meeting. The rendezvous of life and death was a private matter, at least until Joe got back to his home in Grandville and rejoined his wife, Evelyn, and their three teenagers. He forced himself not to rehearse the story of his hunt before it unfolded. He had made that mistake before.

Finally the buck was close enough that Joe began hearing the light crunch in the crisp, dry leaves that a large four-footed animal makes as it walks through the woods. The sound sort of "faded up," as if controlled by the volume button on a TV remote. He considered it a nice change, for once, to not be surprised by the distinct noise. On many occasions, that telltale crunch had shocked him into a state of alertness as quickly as a dentist's probe pressing into a cavity. But whether it came gradually or by surprise, it was hearing that sweet and exciting sound that caused Joe to return to the woods as often as he could.

At 35 yards out and still approaching his position, the deer suddenly stopped and raised its head. Joe was concerned. *Which one of the deer's senses was alerted?* he asked himself silently. It didn't appear that the buck's hearing was aroused because its ears weren't independently twisting like radar. *Did he see something?* Joe wondered. Moving only his eyes from side to side, he scanned the woods and saw nothing unusual in his field of view. *Maybe something is behind me.*

Joe's joy returned when the deer relaxed, but it lasted only a moment. This time the old buck revealed one of the reasons he had survived five or six deer seasons in the Giles County hillsides. He raised his nose to the sky and sniffed the air. He knew something was out of order. Joe's confidence in the procedure he had used to eliminate his own revealing human scent was beginning to dwindle. He had showered with scentless soap. He had stored his camouflage clothes in tightly sealed bags of dried oak leaves for weeks before the season opened. His rubber boots were well seasoned. Still, the buck seemed wary. *What did I forget?* Joe worriedly asked himself. He knew that the nose of an experienced deer could detect anything from the lingering smell of toothpaste to the faint aroma of oil drops clinging to a knife blade that's been sharpened on a whetstone. He decided he'd done his homework as best he could. The old storehouse of intelligence that stood on four legs beneath him was simply trained by time—and other humans—to sense something unusual in his presence.

The sight of the big buck was reason enough for all of Joe's senses to go into overload and refuse to cooperate. However, in that incredible moment, somewhere deep within, he was experiencing a strange calm. It wasn't a poise that settled the fleshly nerves because he was still extremely excited—and his wildly racing heart proved it. Instead, it was a peace based on knowledge gained through experience. He had practiced shooting his bow for hours in his backyard. He had destroyed a 3D target and totally unraveled a burlap bag of rags with hundreds of shots. He knew how to hit a mark. He was prepared in the art of picking a spot on the deer and concentrating on it. He was ready!

He was also aware that he had to overcome the temptation to look too long at the antlers. Past encounters with that thief of concentration, which Joe laughingly called "the rack attack," had taught him well. It was a fatal distraction, one he knew took serious discipline to avoid. He had learned that in order to maintain steady emotions, he could not allow his eyes to wander away from the area behind the shoulder of the deer.

Finally, and most important of all, his calmness was rooted in an inward resolve that no matter what transpired in the minutes that followed it had already been a great day in the woods. He was determined to simply enjoy his participation in the course of events that was soon to pass.

With his attitude correctly in place, Joe cautiously checked the arrow's position on the bow's rest. He glanced at the finger tab on his right hand to make sure it was properly placed on the string. Then, once again, he mentally went through the steps to full draw. All that remained was to wait patiently for the deer to turn its body broadside and present a shot that would allow him to put its vitals in his peep sight.

The deer finally took a few steps. Whatever the scent might have been that caught his attention earlier, it was apparently not dangerous enough to make him run. Still, the buck's gait was slow and deliberate, the kind of movement a whitetail makes that informs the hunter that his window of opportunity is closing. The deer suddenly stopped, stood broadside about 25 yards away, and looked straight toward the tree that held Joe's stand. He knew that to make any attempt to move when there was nothing between him and the deer's eyes was a fruitless endeavor. In some cases, all it took was an odd shape or an unfamiliar silhouette to cause a deer to spook and run away. He had to trust that the dark-brown and green face paint around his eyes, his mesh camo face mask, his camo clothes and hat, and the placement of the treestand were doing their job in fooling the buck's skillful eyes.

What happened next fostered some very mixed feelings in Joe's heart. In all the years he had hunted, he had come to love a great number of things about the process. However, there were some elements that could be quite irritating. Pretty, little, annoying creatures such as chipmunks and squirrels that could detect his presence in the woods and tattle on him had left him very frustrated at times. Then there were the harebrained hunters who, without permission to be on the property, would wander under his stand, fully aware they were trespassing yet offering no apology. Add to that the pesky gnats and mosquitoes that could drive a person crazy. He had suffered many exits from the woods poked full of itching holes and feeling defeated by nature's tiny-winged terrors.

But that morning, one of the most dreaded destroyers of any good hunt made itself known—a dog. From the hillside behind the buck, about 400 yards away, came a series of healthy yelps. Joe whispered silently, *Oh, no! The canine curse!*

The unexpected sound of the barking intruder turned out to be the welcomed voice of "man's best friend" this time. Joe was surprised to find himself basking in the glow of the disturbance when the noise made the deer bristle and turn its head to look in the dog's direction. With the buck's eyes looking away, Joe quickly and quietly lifted his bow out of the short holster that hung from his belt and came to full draw.

"Pick a spot" was all he allowed himself to think. As he looked through the tiny hole in his peep sight, he focused on the white 20-yard pin. To allow for the extra distance that the arrow would have to travel, he placed it on a spot about 4 inches above the heart area of the big buck. Joe let go of the string, and the bow recoiled in his left hand. Within an instant, the neon green-and-yellow plastic fletching on the rear of the aluminum arrow disappeared into the deer's brownish fur. The woods exploded. Leaves and dirt flew up under the buck's hooves as he kicked high, wheeled around, then headed out of sight down the ridge from whence he had come.

Fifteen to 20 seconds passed, and silence fell once again in the forest. Joe longed to hear the crashing sound that a deer makes when it expires on a "dead run" and piles up onto the forest floor. However, there was only unsettling stillness. He was confident that his broadhead arrow tip had done its deed, but he also knew that the buck was strong, smart, and scared enough to go as far as he could from where he had encountered the sudden pain.

Joe was surprised at first that the deer chose to run toward the dog, but then he reasoned, *Who, or what, would be thinking clearly if there was a sudden stinging in the chest?* He assumed the buck had somehow gathered its senses, took the canine's presence into consideration, and somewhere made a turn. The hunter's only hope was for a good blood trail.

2

＞—◆＞—０—＜◆—＞—＜

As Joe passed through the first two minutes following the shot, a thousand thoughts went through his mind, but none took root. He stood amid swirling emotions, kind of like the feelings that settle in on a person after he has barely avoided a serious car accident. Calm at first, then, about three miles down the highway, reality returns and the awareness of what could have happened causes the legs to grow weak, the hands to shake, and the palms to drip with sweat. Feeling no less rattled in the excitement generated by the encounter with the big buck, all Joe could do was sit down on his treestand seat and wait for a normal heartbeat to return. He was loving every minute of it!

After he carefully replayed the shot over and over in his mind and was sure it was a good hit, Joe put his head back on the tree bark and took a deep breath. At the end of a lengthy sigh, he gritted his teeth, clenched his fist, and quietly screamed a word he had often heard his 16-year-old son say after sinking a long, three-point shot on the basketball court: *"Yes!"* It felt so good, he said it again. *"Yes!"* Then he looked through the leaves above him into the brilliant-blue October sky and whispered a prayer of deep gratitude. "Thank You, Lord!"

Caution argued with instinct as Joe fought the urge to immediately begin a search for the buck. He knew if there was any life at all in the animal, it would not hesitate to flee at the sight or sound of an over-anxious hunter. As a result, his post-shot procedure was tried and true. If he saw the deer go down, he waited 15 minutes before leaving his stand. If it went down and audibly crashed in the leaves but out of the range of his eyes, he allowed 45 minutes to pass before finding the deer. If the animal disappeared completely out of sight, and no sound was heard that indicated it fell onto the forest floor, he waited at least an hour. Knowing that the next 60 minutes would pass at a snail's pace, he forced himself to relax.

Joe checked the time and began his vigil. To pass the minutes, he decided to start with a snack. His 46-year-old heart would not allow him the delicious luxury of a chocolate bar—one too many sweet celebrations in the past had yielded a stern warning from his doctor. His compliance to a better diet was made easier, however, when, during one visit, the doctor said, "If you want to keep climbing into those trees and terrorizing Bambi's daddy, you'd better tend to your ticker!" That was all it took. Joe changed his dietary ways. As he sat in his physician's waiting room and reluctantly read the low-fat rules he had to follow, he couldn't help but wonder if Evelyn had put those words of warning in his doctor's mouth. He knew his wife loved him enough to pull that kind of trick. At any rate, for a snack an apple had to do.

Then there was the matter of completing the big game tag attached to his license. He dug into his shirt pocket for his pen and started to fill it out, but then decided to wait. He knew it wasn't wise to count his points before they were mounted. Instead, he decided to lower his bow to the ground and climb down from the treestand. He attached his light-brown lowering string to the end of his bow and then hesitated. *What if that deer is only wounded and disoriented enough to wander back by me? It's happened before! I'd better sit right here and wait!* he thought.

As he again sat quietly and absorbed the sounds of the mid-morning woods, Joe's mind drifted from thought to thought for the 45 minutes that remained. His attention first went to Bob Gleason and how kind the elderly gentleman was to permit him to hunt on his 800 acres. The land had been in the Gleason family for nearly 100 years. Joe's heart was saddened by the fact that Bob was a widower. His wife of nearly 50 years took ill with a lung disease and died, leaving him alone in their big two-story white house. Bob didn't allow the place to change much, inside or out, in order to preserve his fond memories of the woman he cherished so greatly. His attention was especially directed at maintaining the flower garden Sarah had so carefully created. It was his show of respect for her beauty, which he loved to remember.

The wood-frame house was a handful to take care of, but Bob valued his chores since they helped occupy his thoughts and time. Joe considered his assistance with odd jobs around the farm, like mowing the fields and cutting firewood, both emotional therapy and a grand opportunity to show good faith as a land user.

Joe looked at the trees that surrounded him and imagined what tales they could tell about the four Gleason kids who once played in the woods where he sat. He also wondered which of them might be the next to surprise their father by showing up unannounced. Bob's children were very good about coming in to see him and keeping tabs on his bachelorhood.

Then, for some reason, Earl Potter came to Joe's mind. He was an unmarried man, somewhat aloof, and Joe had never been able to get to know him as well as he would like. Earl had moved into the area a little over four years ago. A younger gentleman in his late 30s, he seemed to be a good neighbor to Bob. He was at the Gleason home when Sarah said farewell to her husband and children. Before she passed away, Sarah freely told everyone in earshot, including Earl, how Jesus had gotten her "all cleaned up inside and ready for heaven," and He wanted to do the same for everyone she knew. Earl politely endured her preaching, but to Joe's knowledge he had never accepted the "gospel according to Sarah." Bob had expressed a time or two how grateful he was that Earl was nearby.

Joe's memories of Sarah were priceless treasures in his heart. He had a bond with that old saint that could not be severed by her passing. He knew he would see her again someday, and he smiled at the comforting thought that with her new body, Sarah could breathe deeply with no trouble. As his Sunday school teacher, she had instructed him in his impressionable years, and the seed of eternal hope in the Savior took root and bore good fruit in Joe's late teens. He wondered if she somehow knew he was thinking about her as the time ticked by in his treestand. Only 17 minutes remained in the wait.

Joe rummaged through his pockets to make sure he had the hot-pink plastic ribbon he used for tracking the blood trail he hoped he would find. As he did so, he had a few more interesting thoughts. One, if he found the deer, what would his two hunting buddies say when they saw it? He knew what L.D. Hill would do. He would drop to his knees, as if bowing to a king, and pay homage to the hunter. That was L.D.'s comical way of congratulating his comrades on their hunting success. He did it even if the deer was antlerless. Joe's carpenter friend believed that any animal that was taken with a bow and arrow and headed to the freezer was a trophy. Joe liked and shared L.D.'s attitude.

Then there was Bill Foster, the Southern gentleman bank manager, a transplant from the rolling hills of Georgia. Joe loved Bill's "mountain manners." When Bill saw the deer, he would just grunt and spit. Joe chuckled when he recalled the day they'd first met. It was in the halls of their old high school, and Bill was a new arrival. Joe looked at his 6'4" frame, peered up into his eyes, and jokingly said, "Would you do me a favor? Please...don't ever get mad at me!" Bill innocently assumed he was serious and answered with a gentle voice and a drawn-out Southern accent, "All...right!"

Joe's thoughts turned somber as he recalled what had happened the night before in his hometown of Grandville. Having a population of around 8,000, the peaceful little town wasn't used to the kind of violence it had experienced. Near closing time, two armed men entered Harper's Grocery and demanded the day's cash earnings. When a patron named Phillip Simpson attempted to squelch the robbery, the two thieves made their intentions perfectly clear when one of them buried a round from a heavy-caliber pistol into the would-be hero. The assailants made off with a significant amount of cash. At newstime on the regional TV station, it was reported that Simpson was in very critical condition at the county hospital; his chances of survival were dangerously slim.

Joe didn't know the bystander, but he whispered a prayer for the man and his family. The whole matter was depressing, and it didn't help to know the criminals had escaped. That unwelcome news was confirmed when Joe had passed through a police roadblock at 4:15 on his way to the Gleason farm. Trooper Lance Wilson had greeted him at his driver's window.

"How are you doing, Mr. Tanner? I guess you know why we're out here at this hour."

"Yes, I know," Joe responded.

"I bet you're going hunting. Am I right?"

"You bet!"

"Well, the good news is that the suspects were reported to be heading in the opposite direction from where you're going."

"That's what I heard last night. Otherwise, I wouldn't be out here at this time of the morning. Evelyn, my wife, would have never allowed it," Joe admitted with a smile.

As he started to drive away, he was offered one last word of advice by the tired officer. "Be careful, Mr. Tanner."

When he pulled away, Joe looked into his rearview mirror and saw Trooper Wilson's face glowing like a crimson ghost in the red glow of the taillights. A little farther down the road he slowly passed under the protective illumination of the last street lamp at the edge of Grandville. With the comfort of the city lights fading behind him, he looked ahead into the thick blackness of the predawn countryside…and shivered at the thought of the two dangerous men roaming free in his area.

3

The hour wait finally ended and the bell inside Joe's head sounded to begin the search for the deer. Joe stood, stretched like a waking house cat, and began the dismount process. First, he took his waist pack off the tree limb where it had been hanging and buckled it around his trim waist. Then he lowered his bow and quiver to the ground with his 20 feet of strong cord. He unbuckled his safety belt, carefully put his weight onto the screw-in steps implanted into the tree, and descended the 18 feet. After detaching his bow from the pull-up rope, he turned to face the challenge of recovering the deer.

Joe carefully walked over to the area where the buck had stood broadside just over an hour earlier. Hoping the arrow had passed completely through the deer, he peered into the leaves looking for the brightly colored fletching. "Aha!" he whispered excitedly when, just four steps away, he saw a mere inch or so of the neon green plastic glowing like a beacon among the mix of brown and rust-colored leaves. His hand shook as he pulled the arrow out of the soft dirt beneath the leafy, autumn blanket. He held the aluminum shaft at eye level and there it was…dried blood! The sight always sent a chill up his spine, reflecting the mingling of joy and sorrow. He was joyful knowing his arrow had found its mark, but he felt sorrow in knowing that he had inflicted such pain on an animal so awesome. The two feelings were never separated in Joe's heart, and he knew if they ever were he would never go hunting again.

For nearly 30 minutes he slowly followed a trail of blood drops and torn-up forest floor. He marked every find of blood by tying a four-inch portion of the pink ribbon to nearby branches. Finally, he looked back through the woods at the line of pink that was formed by his markers. It revealed that the deer had run straight for about 60 yards, and then turned slightly to the right and headed downhill toward a cedar thicket.

Joe's experience with the tracking process demanded that he not get anxious. Still, he struggled to maintain his composure. He knew there was plenty of daylight remaining, and there was no need to hurry—except for the fact that he had made a firm promise to Evelyn that he'd be home before lunch to complete some very important items on her "honey do" list.

Ten yards ahead was a sign that the buck was slowing. It appeared that it had lain down for a moment. However, the strong animal had managed to stand up and walk on. Joe talked to himself: *Stay calm. Don't break the rules. Be smart, keep your eyes to the ground, and think red.*

Bent over like an inspector with a magnifying glass, Joe studied the earth and took another seven or eight steps. When he stood upright to rest his back, his heart leaped as he looked about 20 yards ahead. First he saw the dark-brown fur, then he saw one side of a 22-inch spread hovering parallel to the ground. As he nocked an arrow, he watched the deer for a moment to check for the rise and fall of its ribcage. Though it seemed the buck was down for good, he lifted his bow and prepared to quickly come to full draw just to be safe. He gingerly stepped forward.

As he slowly walked up to the deer, his first guess was 160 to 170 pounds. "What an animal!" Joe said out loud. Confident the deer had expired, he relaxed his arms. A great sense of relief filled his mind with the realization that recovery had been accomplished, and there would be no need to return after dark with a lantern to track the deer. Joe had been through enough all-night searches for wounded animals to

teach him to stay out of trouble when it came to shooting and tracking a whitetail.

His skills, which yielded the 10-point buck that lay at his feet, were
a product of his early years spent in the woods with his dad and uncles
as they schooled him in the art of hunting. Joe's dad was well-known
in the area for his record-book whitetail whose antlers hung on the wall
at Jim's Quickmart on the east side of town. It sported 27 points and
proudly held a place in the *Boone & Crockett* record book. The mount
attracted tourists, which helped business at Jim's market, especially in
the fall of the year when the "deer season juices" started to flow in hunters' hearts. After his dad lost a battle with cancer at the young age of 62,
Joe memorialized him as a local hero of the woods by hanging a plaque
and his dad's picture beneath the large mount. The inscription read:

Taken by JOSEPH M. TANNER, Sr.
27 points / Nov. 16, 1964
Largest deer ever taken in Giles County

As the 10 o'clock hour arrived in the Gleason woods, Joe knelt on
one knee next to the big buck and took a moment to admire his prize.
As he did, he thought of a talk his father had given him one morning
while driving in an old Chevy pickup to a nearby farm to deer hunt.
With both hands on the wheel and bouncing in the seat as the old
truck rolled over the bumpy, dirt road, Joe's dad began to pass along
his whitetail wisdom to his attentive son.

"If you're going to find a deer, you have to think like a deer. Watch
him and learn his habits. Get a good idea of what his next move will be.
Use every hunt to learn more about the animal. Let your failures teach
you how to be successful."

His dad continued. "Remember, deer always feel hunted. Why
do you think their heads bob up and down when they're feeding? It's
because they don't trust anything. They always assume there's danger
nearby. It's in their nature, and that's why they can live so long. The
more caution they have, the longer they live. Also, deer can be patient.
They can outwait you. They don't have to hurry home…or hurry to

anywhere. They're home already. They just wander back and forth from their kitchen to their bedroom. Humans can't stand to be motionless for very long, and it seems like whitetail know it. They'll let you make the mistake!

"Son," Joseph, Sr. went on, "just imagine being hunted. I guarantee you'll learn to be alert. Surviving is a deer's job. In order to outsmart him, you have to utilize his distractions. There are two things that can cause a buck to forget his cautious nature. One is his belly. They love to eat. They not only like the taste of corn and acorns and such, they also know instinctively that they have to store up for the long winter. So we hunt their belly in the early part of the season. Then later on in the year, when 'love' begins to call, a buck forgets about his belly and thinks about the babes!"

Joe's dad couldn't bring himself to fully explain the sex drive that takes over the buck's ability to think clearly. He finally said to his youthful and innocent son, "Just keep this in mind, young man. If you're not careful, chasing girls can sometimes give you a lot of trouble. You'll know what I mean in a few years!"

Joe smiled as he thought of how modest and tender his father was, yet how tough he had been when he needed to be strong. His heart was saddened at the thought that his dad couldn't see this 10-point. Suddenly a breeze of divine joy swept through Joe's heart. *Then again...perhaps he does see this trophy!*

4

✂ ►•◄►•O•◄►•◄ ✂

Ahead of Joe was his least favorite part of the hunt. It was the process his dad and uncles called "gutting" the deer. While some modern hunters chose to delicately refer to it as "field dressing" the animal, Joe knew that even with a nice title, it would still be a messy, smelly affair. The one thing that redeemed the unpleasant chore was imagining the tasty dishes Evelyn would create out of the carefully prepared meat.

With his sharp, single-blade hunting knife, Joe made a long cut through the skin of the deer's underside. He removed his blaze-orange, shoulder-length plastic gloves from his waist pack and put them on. They would protect his hands and arms from the bloody mess as he reached in to remove the entrails. Suddenly a cold chill shivered through his body. He remembered what a Giles County man had experienced the year before during archery season. The hunter had taken a large doe, then searched the woods thoroughly for his arrow. But he hadn't found it…until the moment he was doing exactly what Joe was about to do. The front part of the shaft had broken off in the deer's lung area, leaving the razor-sharp broadhead inside. When the man drug his palm across the three blades, it had cut his hand so severely that he nearly lost the use of it. Joe decided it was better to be safe than sorry, so he removed the used arrow from the quiver and checked to see that all the blades were still mounted to it. Satisfied that it was safe to continue, he completed the task at hand.

Joe couldn't help but anticipate Evelyn's standard reaction when he delivered a deer. He knew she would put both hands on her hips and take a stance like a pioneer woman might have taken as she looked across an ancient prairie. Then she would say in a primitive style, "You kill! Me cook!" He couldn't wait to hear it.

To experience her verbal reward, Joe had to take on the most strenuous part of harvesting a deer—he had to get the animal to his truck. Worst of all, he had no help. Hunting alone was not Joe's preference, especially when there was dragging to be done. Fortunately, the big buck had fallen a tolerable distance from the unpaved county road where the truck was parked. Joe was also pleased when he realized the drag would be downhill a good part of the way.

After 15 minutes of vigorous pulling on the limp body of the heavy buck and several rest stops later, Joe was within 25 yards of the road. He left the deer inside the edge of the woods, stepped into the open lane, turned right, and began the quarter-mile walk to his pickup.

The full-size truck was, as his two teenage daughters put it, "his four-wheeled friend." It was indeed a welcomed sight as he rounded the bend in the road a few minutes later. His old truck hadn't had the luxuries this new one sported. He was especially grateful for the king cab that provided so much space behind his driver's seat. There he stored important items, including his spare bow with a quiver full of arrows.

Joe lowered the tailgate, turned around, and sat down. When his aching back and tired muscles felt the much-needed rest, he moaned with a sigh of relief. As he took off his bloody gloves and wiped away the salty sweat that ran down his forehead, he laughingly commented, "Deer hunting is hard work, but somebody has to do it!" He thought of how many of his friends at the aluminum plant where he worked would love to be where he was at the moment. Feeling quite blessed with the hunt he had enjoyed, he removed his waist pack and laid it aside. He put his bow on top of its unopened soft case in the truck bed then closed the gate. What a happy sound it was to his ears when the new 8-cylinder engine roared to life. With his mission nearing completion, Joe turned the truck around and headed down the gravel road toward his waiting trophy.

On the short drive to the deer, Joe wondered how he would get the big animal into the bed of his truck. As the air conditioner offered a momentary respite from the midday autumn warmth, he decided to enjoy the challenge and try to keep from permanently injuring his back. All in all, he was happy to have the problem that lay ahead.

As he backed the blue-and-white 4-wheel drive to the spot where he'd left the deer, Joe remembered he hadn't tagged the buck. It was a detail he was ashamed to have forgotten. He felt safe in leaving the deer where it was, since only a few folks were allowed to hunt the area. Still, he was not one to forget too many steps in the process. He also realized he had not called home to touch base with Evelyn. It was a rigid routine he'd developed that his wife deeply appreciated since hunting had its share of dangers. Since he was just a few short minutes from leaving, he decided to wait and make the call after the deer was loaded and tagged.

Joe turned off the motor and opened the door. Out of habit, he pulled the keys from the ignition and slipped them into his right front pants pocket. Then he put on gloves that were rubber beaded in the palms and walked to the large deer. Grabbing it by the antlers, he happily grunted as he drug it the few remaining yards to the truck. The 4-wheel-drive chassis made the tailgate look like it was two stories off the ground as Joe stood over the huge deer and surveyed the challenge ahead.

"I'll never get this beast in the bed of this truck by myself!" Joe mumbled. He was not about to be defeated, though. Muscling the head of the buck onto the tailgate, the rest of the deer's body dangled onto the ground. As he held it in place for a moment and planned his next move, he was surprised by a voice that came from nearby.

"Looks like you could use some help, mister!"

Joe felt a little embarrassed that another hunter had caught him in the midst of an attempt to seriously impair himself, so he didn't look up, but responded, "Yes, sir. Your timing is perfect!"

Then a second voice added, "Yeah, he'll be *glad* we came along!"

As Joe lowered the heavy head and rack of antlers back onto the ground, he peered around his truck to see his unexpected visitors. Their faces were not familiar, but he was not about to refuse help from anyone at this point. One of the men was dressed in old blue jeans and a well-worn army camo-type jacket. He had a mustache and a thin strip of dark beard that ran downward from the center of his lower lip and under his chin. The other had on a brown leather waistlength coat with big pockets and dark-colored jeans. Both were wearing baseball caps and tennis shoes. Their hair seemed unkempt and oily.

Joe was a little puzzled at their attire and mentally assessed the reason for their presence. *Are they hunters?* he wondered. He immediately dismissed that possibility since they were without archery equipment. *Perhaps these guys are power company employees out here working on the...*

Joe suddenly stopped in midthought. He swallowed hard and his blood ran cold. His heart started beating in his chest with a rhythm faster than any deer's presence had ever generated. His hands began to shake. He knew who the two men were!

5

❦

"So, you gonna let us help you load that deer?" one of the men asked.

In the face of his building emotions, Joe struggled to quickly think of a response that would not only be diversionary, but one that would also sound convincing. "Well, obviously I can use your help, but I sure wouldn't want you to get your clothes all messy. I have a buddy, L.D., who I'm hopin' will come by any minute now and help me out, but I guess we can get the job started."

Joe's hopes that the two unwelcome strangers would assume that he was not alone faded quickly. His plan was shattered when one of the men said to his partner, "Man, I think we're lookin' at our ticket back to the big city!"

Joe didn't hesitate. Seeing they had no weapons in hand, he suddenly wheeled around on his heels, ran into the woods, and disappeared into the dense brush. He left the two men standing there completely bewildered and surprised by his quick actions.

"Let him go!" Jack yelled as his partner felt for his .357 pistol. Joe clearly heard the loud command as he quietly fought his way up the hill. He knew the woods very well and was aware that the crest of the slope he was climbing was about 200 yards ahead. He took his steps cautiously but quickly, trying to be as quiet as possible.

With smug confidence, one of the men walked to the cab of the truck and stood with his arms outstretched, admiring Joe's truck. "Man, this baby's brand-new! We can go in style. It's even a 4-wheel drive. We'll be able to…"

The other man stopped his partner in the middle of his commentary. "Hey, Shelby! Check the ignition. Hurry! Are the keys in it?"

Shelby quickly opened the driver's door and rubbernecked a look at the ignition. Finding it empty, he cursed under his breath and then hollered, "He's got the keys, Jack!"

"We've gotta find him!" Jack immediately decided. "He can't be that far away."

Both of them quickly reached into their coat pockets and pulled out matching chrome-plated .357 magnum Smith & Wessons. They started to follow Joe's path into the woods, but Jack hesitated. "Wait. We've gotta disable this truck in case that moron circles around and comes back here. He might have the keys, but we'll take us a little prize along that will stop him."

Shelby agreed. "Good idea!" He reached up under the dash, pulled the hood lever, and ran around to the engine compartment. He found the ignition coil wire harness and quickly detached it from its place. As he stuffed it into his coat pocket he bragged, "It'll turn over, but it won't fire!"

Jack rushed around to the tailgate while Shelby was disabling the truck. He discovered Joe's compound bow with its attached quiver full of arrows. "We'll disarm this guy too!" Jack grabbed the bow by the lower limb and gave it an angry fling. It sailed like a Frisbee into the high weeds on the opposite side of the gravel road.

By the time the two men had discovered there were no keys in the truck and had tossed away their new victim's defenses, Joe had the few precious minutes he needed to make it to a cedar thicket where he knew he could hide. He stopped briefly to listen, but his heart was pumping hard and his blood rushing so fast it was difficult to hear anything other than his own breathing. He turned an ear to the road below, straining to catch the sound of his truck rolling away on the gravel. As much as he liked his pickup, the thought of it being the victim instead of himself was much more appealing. Right now he only cared about seeing Evelyn and their three kids once again.

Joe pulled his left shirt sleeve up to check the time and discovered his watch wasn't there. Suddenly he remembered it was in the place he always put it when in the treestand to muffle any of its unexpected and untimely chirps. He dug into his right pants pocket to retrieve it and as he did, he felt the unmistakable clump of metal keys. His pulse skyrocketed even higher than it already was.

Oh no! I have what they want! He could feel his knees grow weak as he realized that since he had seen their faces he could identify them as well. *That's why I haven't heard them drive away! They're gonna come after the truck keys…and me!*

He looked at his watch, but he could barely read it due to his shaking hand. Finally he figured out it was 10:35. He knew it wouldn't take too long before Evelyn would begin to feel concerned if he didn't show up at home or at least call with an adjusted schedule. He hated the thought of worrying the woman he loved so much.

As his mind raced through his options, Joe checked his pockets for anything he might use in the situation that had turned very serious. Along with his keys, in his right pants pocket he had a small Swiss Army knife that had one short main blade. He carried it primarily for the toothpick, as well as the Phillip's head and flat screwdriver for emergency bow repairs. He wished for the bigger knife he had used for field dressing the deer, but it was in the truck bed wrapped up in the bloody, orange gloves for later cleaning.

In the left pocket of his camo pants was his remaining 30 feet of pink tracking ribbon and his finger tab. In the lower right knee pocket of his pants, he found the long string he used to raise and lower his bow out of the treestand. In his left shirt pocket was a black indelible ink pen, his hunting license, and his deer tag. As he stuffed the waterproof paper forms back into his shirt pocket, Joe wondered if the deer he left behind would ever wear the tag that would officially document the existence of such a massive creature.

As he continued to wait in the cedar thicket, listening for the crunch of leaves or the breaking of twigs on the forest floor, Joe hoped the two culprits would not be able to hide their movements. His ears perked up when he heard the crackling sound of dry wood in the distance.

Jack whispered, "We'll have to be quiet. This guy's a hunter!"

Shelby confidently responded, "We'll find him...and we'll drop him like that buck layin' behind the pickup!"

"You're gonna have to watch where you're walkin'!" Jack demanded quietly a few minutes later as the weight of Shelby's foot broke a limb buried in the leaves.

"I'm doin' the best I can, Jack. What do you expect? Besides...you're not doin' much better. You sound like you're walkin' on cornflakes!"

When Joe figured out where the sound was coming from, it occurred to him that the two men were far enough away from the road that he could probably circle back, get in his truck, and drive to safety.

"This is my chance!" he quietly whispered. He resisted standing fully upright as he carefully chose each step, desperately trying to avoid the snap of fallen limbs under his boots.

Ten minutes later, Joe's thighs burned and his knees ached as he "duck walked" his way to within sight of the blue-and-white truck. He crawled to a position only 50 yards from his vehicle and waited, motionless, on his knees. He watched the area carefully to see if there was any movement. When he was satisfied that both men were still in the woods looking for him, he crawled snakelike toward his pickup.

At the edge of the woods, he waited another minute and watched the area. His heart pounded nearly out of control as he retrieved his keys from his pocket and quickly ran to the truck and squatted on the driver's side. In one motion, he opened the door, climbed in, slid behind the steering wheel, and softly closed the door behind him. His nervous fingers fumbled in his attempt to slide the key into the ignition. As he looked quickly from side to side, scanning the edge of the woods through the windows of the truck, he turned the key expecting the engine to roar to life. It refused to fire. He tried again. Nothing. His heart sank when he looked out the front windshield and saw the partially closed hood. Guessing the two men had done something to disable his new truck, he coaxed himself, "Don't panic ole buddy. They'll be back here any second. You'd better do something fast!"

Nervously forgetting for a moment which of the Tanner family vehicles he was in, Joe frantically searched for the door handle. "We have too many cars!" he grumbled. Finally he found the latch, gave it a jerk, and the door flew open. Before he exited, he once again, out of habit, pulled his keys out of the ignition and stuffed them into his pocket. Quickly he ran to the bed of the truck to grab his bow and quiver before heading back into the woods. He was surprised and disgusted when he rounded the tailgate and saw that the bow was gone.

Doubt and despair showed no mercy to Joe's emotions as he thought of having no way to defend himself. Suddenly, a ray of hope returned when he remembered what was in his new truck's extended cab. "Aha! My old back-up bow!" He ran to the open driver's door, grabbed the "seat forward" lever, and slid the bench toward the dash, making room to reach for his bow that was wrapped carefully in a protective blanket. Laying next to it was his detachable quiver that held four arrows tipped with field points, which he used for target practice. He wished for something more substantial, but he would have to do without razor-tipped arrows.

As he pulled the bow and quiver from the cab and quietly snapped them together, he caught sight of another item he knew he could use—his phone. He quickly grabbed it and tucked it into the knee pocket of his pants.

Feeling sure that time was much too short before the two maniacs returned, Joe decided to abandon his search for more things that might have made the situation more favorable for him. With his left hand holding the bow, Joe used his right hand to quietly bring the door to its closed position. He then crouched and quickly ran to the edge of the woods, vanishing once again.

6

"Hold it!" Jack shouted.

Shelby halted in mid-stride. "What is it, Jack?"

"Listen!"

In the distance they heard the engine in Joe's truck try to turn over.

"Let's go!" Shelby called as he turned and ran toward the road. Jack followed and within 90 seconds they were within sight of the truck. With pistols cupped in both hands ready to fire, the two of them carefully approached the lifeless pickup. Shelby checked the ignition, and once again found it keyless.

Jack nervously paced back and forth a couple of times beside the truck. "Shelby, see if you can hot-wire this thing. I'll keep watch."

"I don't think so, Jack. These newfangled trucks are so computerized that without a degree in mechanics, it's tough to get one of 'em going."

"Just try it, Shelby! What have we got to lose?" Jack shouted as he looked up and down the road.

"Time! That's what we've got to lose, Jack! There are so many anti-theft devices on these new models, it's useless for me to even try to mess with it."

Jack kicked the gravel on the road in frustration. "This guy has seen us! We can't let him see us again—especially in a line-up. We'll just have to split up and find him. We'll waste him, get the keys, get back to the bridge, get the cash, and get out of here!"

"Sounds like a plan to me, Jack." Then Shelby added sarcastically, "However, if *your* friend had met us at that bridge last night like he said he would, we wouldn't be sidetracked out here in the middle of nowhere!"

Neither of the two men knew that less than 50 yards away Joe was watching intently, desperately hoping they would give up and leave the area. Joe swallowed hard in disbelief that he was seeing the same guns that had critically wounded Phillip Simpson the night before being readied to be used against him.

Evelyn looked at the clock on the microwave above the oven, slightly raised her eyebrows, and offered a subdued, "Hmmmm." With all that Joe had on the docket to do for the remainder of their day, it surprised her that he was nearly an hour late. He was usually very faithful about letting her know if he was running late, especially since the welcomed introduction of the smart phone. On a rare occasion or two, however, he had been known to suddenly appear unannounced at their back door, two or three hours past his predicted return. She knew what to expect when it happened. Joe would grovel in repentance, then encourage her to go outside and view his gift of venison to the family. He would stand there in a humble, yet comical way, and wait for her to congratulate him for his success as a provider. It was a ritual that Evelyn enjoyed and quietly anticipated as she looked once again at the clock and resumed her work.

Bob Gleason's phone rang and a voice on the other end followed his greeting with, "Hey, Bob, this is L.D. How are you doin'?"

"I'm fine, L.D. How are you and your bunch?"

"We're all doin' fine. Summer's hangin' on this year, ain't it?"

"Sure is, my friend. But I tell you, driving on dust is a lot easier than driving on ice!"

"Well, Bob, you're always lookin' on the bright side of things." L.D.

was grateful that his seasoned friend was sounding strong. He continued, "Say, Bob, I've got some free time this afternoon, and I wondered if you'd mind if me and my boy, Stan, came and wet our hooks in your pond?"

"I wish you would, L.D. This old water hole needs a good purging. The bass are gonna get stunted in their growth. I sure do hope you like bluegill, too. There's still a bunch of 'em!"

L.D. answered with a thankful tone. "Bob, I'm not picky. I even like tadpoles if they're bitin'! We'll be there in about an hour, and we'll stop in and say howdy!"

Joe quietly took the phone out of his knee pocket and nervously covered the speaker with the palm of his hand to muffle the power-up beep. The battery showed plenty of life, but his hope that the meter would show a strong enough signal to make a 911 call was dampened when the "no service" message appeared in the small window of the phone.

I'll have to wait till I get to the top of the hill to make the call, he thought as he once again palmed the speaker and pushed the off button. *I'd sure like to leave this thing on, but as sure as the world, it would ring at the worst time.*

As the two strangers stood on the opposite side of the truck and quickly planned their pursuit of the man with the keys, Joe decided it was time to slowly move away from his vantage point and carefully head up the forested hillside. The wind was slight, not enough to cover the sound of a twig snapping under his boots, nor was it strong enough to mask the movement of the brush he had to gingerly move away in front of him. Every motion had to be smooth and deliberate.

I can beat these guys, I know it! he thought, as he cautiously stepped over the trunk of a downed beech tree. Then, as high as his confidence soared the moment before, that's how low he fell into despair as the possibility of dodging bullets ravaged his thoughts. He had never been in such a demanding situation. The reality of the danger he was facing was overwhelming, and he had to force himself not to panic. It felt like a frigid December morning in his soul as he shivered in fear.

"God, please help me!" As he whispered the words, Joe realized it was his first utterance of anything resembling prayer since the ordeal had begun. The comfort that it yielded was much needed, so he continued. "Lord, You said if we needed wisdom we could ask for it and You'd give it. If ever I needed a clear mind, it's now. Show me what to do, and deliver me from the evil that's chasing me. I need Your strength!"

Before an "amen" could be offered, Joe heard the distant slam of the truck door. He assumed the two men were on the move. For a fleeting moment, he thought of the deer that lay at his tailgate. *What a waste!* He hated the emotions he was feeling at that moment. As he was thinking about the big buck, an encouraging thought occurred to him.

That old deer eluded many a hunter for several years. It's my turn now! I'm going to have to think like a whitetail! Those hunters will be surprised that their "buck" just might be shootin' back! As Joe guessed what move the wise old deer might have made at that point, he thought about the cedars, and he knew the thicket they bordered would be the best place to hide.

Two hundred yards away, and out of range of Joe's ears, Jack and Shelby stepped as quietly as they knew how through the brushy forest. "This coat is burnin' me up, Jack. Are you hot?"

"Yeah! I'm drippin' with sweat, but we can't stop. We've gotta find this guy."

"Don't you think it would be good to split up now, Jack? I'm not too crazy about the idea, but maybe it's the best thing to do. One of us will find him, and if either of us takes a shot, the other can come runnin' and help out."

"You're probably right. Since he's not armed, let's split up. You go down the hill and circle back around to the truck. I'll follow this ridge a ways, and then circle back. Keep your eyes peeled, Shelby. He's wearin' camouflage so he won't be easy to spot!"

Shelby turned to start down the hill, looked back at Jack, and winked with an evil eye. He gave his buddy a thumbs-up sign, then stepped squarely on a dry oak limb. It snapped like a .22 rifle shot. As Jack shook his head in disgust at Shelby's clumsiness, Joe's ears came to full attention—like a buck on alert!

7

>-+<>-○-<>+-<

Trooper Wilson was about to turn left on Carter Street when he heard his call numbers on his radio. He grabbed his microphone and pressed the talk button.

"Car 5, go ahead."

"Car 5," Carla responded from the central station, "we just received a call from a Mrs. Evelyn Tanner. She said she was concerned about her husband, Joe Tanner. He's late arriving home from hunting. She said you're acquainted with Mr. Tanner, through the city council. She wants you to contact her at your earliest convenience."

"10-4, central. I'll do it right away."

Wilson pulled his patrol car into a school parking lot, put the shift lever into park, and left the engine running. He picked up his cell phone and dialed the Tanners' number.

"Tanner residence," Evelyn answered.

"Evelyn, this is Trooper Lance Wilson. How are you doing?"

"I'm okay, but I'm concerned about Joe."

"The office told me your husband is late getting home from his hunt. I saw him this morning as he was heading out of town. You haven't heard from him since?"

"No, I haven't," Evelyn said with a tone of relief that she was able to discuss her concern with someone.

"How overdue is he, Evelyn?" Trooper Wilson inquired.

"Well, I know it's probably premature to get you involved at this point, but something is bothering me. Joe is very prompt…and he always checks in if he's going to be late. Right now, he's only about two hours past when he promised he'd be here. Believe me, I wouldn't be calling if there weren't two murderers on the run. It just doesn't add a whole lot of comfort to the situation." Evelyn paused, then continued, "Well…Joe's out there, and I'm terribly worried about him. I'm not ready to file a 'missing person' report, but I did think that in your line of work you'd know if those two men were still on the loose. Should I be concerned?"

Trooper Wilson avoided the disheartening news that the convicts were yet to be apprehended by quickly asking, "I know Joe went west out of town, but where exactly did he go to hunt?"

"He went to Bob Gleason's farm. Do you know where that is? I called out there about 30 minutes ago, and Bob had not seen him."

"I know the Gleason place. Does Joe have a phone with him?"

"Yes, he does. I tried it but got the 'unavailable' message. I know it's working because he charged the battery yesterday. Lance, I just have a bad feeling about this. Can you help me?"

"Yes, Evelyn. I'll see what I can find out. Doesn't Joe have a couple of friends he hunts with?"

"Yes. Their names are L.D. Hill and Bill Foster. I haven't talked to them, but I did talk to Tricia Hill. She said L.D. and their son, Stan, were on their way to the Gleason farm to fish this afternoon. They should be there in a little while."

"Does L.D. have a phone?"

"Yes, but Tricia said it's laying on the kitchen counter."

Hoping to steer Evelyn away from unnecessary worry, Wilson offered a logical guess at the reason for Joe's absence. "Your husband is probably occupied with a deer, and he's gonna be calling you soon. In the meantime, I have a few things to check, then I'll head out to the Gleason farm. I'll contact you before I leave town."

Joe looked at his watch and realized nearly two hours had passed since he first encountered his assailants. He had endured a long sit in the thicket, and his muscles were growing stiff. He thought of working his way through the woods to Bob's house, but since there were two gunmen he wasn't sure which direction to go. Staying put seemed to be the best choice. Outrunning a bullet was a race he knew he could never win. He could stay in the thicket until dark if necessary.

After several minutes had passed, a gnawing need invaded his senses. With a morning packed full of the sweat-producing efforts of killing a deer, field dressing it, and dragging it to his truck, as well as trying not to fall prey to a gunblast, his growing thirst became an overwhelming motivation to move. With his waist pack that held a bottle of fresh water still in the truck, his desperate need for liquids drew his mind to the creek below the ridge, toward the area where the dog had barked that morning. He decided he could stay in the protection of the large thicket and carefully crawl down to the spring-fed stream. Without water he wouldn't last as long as he would need to if it became necessary to run any distance.

Though it was a tight fit, Joe forced the bow over his head, worked it down over one of his shoulders, and began crawling on all fours down the hill, stopping often to listen. As he fought the extreme dryness in his mouth, he whispered to himself, "Only 150 yards or so to go. At this rate, I should be there by next summer!" On his hands and knees, Joe could see farther through the thicket than he could when he was standing. *It's not as cluttered down here. It's no wonder those big bucks love this place,* he thought. After another 50 yards of putting one hand and one knee in front of the other, Joe felt something warm and squishy under his left glove. He pulled it back, looked at the palm, and was relieved to find that it was fresh deer droppings. "Whoa, they must be close!" he whispered. Then, about 20 yards in front of him, he heard the familiar crashing of hooves as two deer bounded from the thicket and ran away.

"Oh, no!" he complained softly. "Those deer are making way too much noise."

Jack stopped when the deer began to thunder through the woods, and Shelby heard the noise as well. Both of them immediately assumed it was their prey. Though several yards apart, they were still in eye contact with each other. Jack quietly but vigorously motioned for Shelby to drop down the hill toward the creek. Before Shelby changed directions, Jack gave him another signal to slow down, and then he put his index finger over his lips in an effort to remind him to be quiet. Shelby returned the okay sign and tiptoed down the hill.

Not aware that the two men were only about 200 yards away, but assuming they had heard the noise, Joe picked up his pace. He cautiously worked his way to within 50 feet of the bank of the cool stream. He slowly stood and looked up and down the openness of the creek bed. Satisfied that it was clear, he cautiously and quickly walked to the edge of the water.

As he knelt down on all fours, he removed his right glove and put his face near the inviting pool. Before three sips were taken, Joe raised his head quickly to check the surrounding area. He realized this movement resembled the way deer reacted when they drank. He felt connected with them in their intense caution. He, too, must weigh every move he made. He whispered to himself, "Deer live like this all the time. This is life on the raw edge!"

Praying that the water was untainted, and that a dead raccoon or some other critter was not floating in the water just upstream, Joe anxiously lowered his head to draw one last satisfying gulp. That's when he heard a terrifying noise. It sounded like a sneeze! Grateful for the warning, Joe knew he had to move quickly, yet quietly.

The best route away from the approaching enemy was up the stream for a short distance and then back into the thicket. Joe carefully stepped into the pool where he'd been satisfying his thirst. The water line was just below his ankle-high, size-10 rubber boots. Three more steps and he'd be in the shallows, walking on the greenish-brown rocks that were about two inches under the clear running water. *Don't slip and fall, ole buddy,* he begged himself. *Take it slow!*

Joe had walked about 20 yards up the creek bed when he noticed an obvious deer trail leading up the bank to the right. It led into some thick brush that looked like a good place to hide. As he put his glove back on his right hand, he thought, *Since I have to act like a deer today,*

I may as well follow their route. At that, he dug the toe of his left boot into the muddy creek bank and followed with his right boot. With a strength that came from the power walks that he and Evelyn shared together, he bounded up the bank and followed the deer trail into the dense foliage.

Another sneeze softly echoed up the creek. Joe wondered why he'd heard no voices arguing about the noise. He listened for another moment, then it dawned on him that the two had probably split up. His level of caution escalated when he realized he had to keep watch in front as well as in back of where he was.

Sit tight for a minute, Joe instructed himself. He decided to crawl away from the deer trail to hide and wait. He found a spot where some high grass rose to meet the first branches of some young elm and maple trees. It provided good cover as well as an excellent vantage point to watch the creek bed. Unfortunately, it was also the home of at least a thousand mosquitoes that hadn't succumbed to the long summer. The creamy camo paint on his face, the mesh mask, and the tightly woven gloves on his hands kept most of the bugs at bay. But a few drilled into his sweaty skin as he knelt into a hiding position. He took the green-and-black painted bow off his shoulder and checked it over carefully. Holding it in his left hand, he removed one of the four aluminum arrows from the quiver and nocked it to the string. As he surveyed the small opening through which he would watch the creek, the chilling thought came to him that he was preparing for battle. A dark cloud of dread came over his heart as he put on his finger tab, placed it on the bowstring, and checked around to see if he had room to come to full draw.

8

⊱─━◆─○─◆━─⊰

As he faced the unbelievable possibility of shooting someone with his bow and arrow, Joe mentally rehearsed his shot. Although he wouldn't attempt to kill either of the criminals, he knew he had to place his arrows well enough to disable them. He felt squeamish at the thought. It was hard for him to imagine what damage even a slender field tip would do to a person, but he was hoping it wouldn't be fatal. Sweat ran off his forehead. He slowly raised his hand and wiped away the salty drops that were beginning to sting his eyes. *What I don't need now is blurred vision.* The tension was building.

L.D. and Stan arrived at the Gleason farm and stopped by Bob's house. They walked onto the huge covered porch and knocked on the door. It took a couple of minutes for it to swing open, and L.D. greeted his elderly friend.

"How's it goin' today, Bob?"

"Still alive, L.D. I see you have your fishin' buddy with you."

"You bet! I'm sure thankful for teachers' meetings, especially when they fall on a beautiful day like this. When Stan is along, the fish seem to jump up on the bank and put the stringer in their mouths. It's fun to watch. I'm sure glad he could come!"

Bob looked at the young man who was basking in the glow of his father's kind words.

"Well, I hope you catch enough fish today to fill up the bed of your dad's old truck. If you need any worms, stop at the barn out back and turn over a few of those old 2 x 10s layin' on the ground. You'll find a whole city of 'em under there." He turned back to L.D. "I'm sorry you had to wait for me to answer the door. Evelyn Turner called. Seems to be worried about Joe."

"What's goin' on with Joe?" L.D. asked.

"Well, he told Evelyn he wanted to be home by eleven this morning, but he hasn't shown up. He came out here to bow hunt today. I told her it might be too early to start pushin' the panic button, but Evelyn said with those two gunmen on the loose, plus the fact that Joe is not one to keep her in the dark, she has an uneasy feeling. You haven't talked to him today, have you?"

"Sure haven't. But I'm with you. I wouldn't worry about Joe. He's probably got somethin' bleedin' out there, and you know deer hunters—when they get on a trail, they lose all track of reality, especially when it comes to schedules! It can even happen to old Mr. Dependable. He might end up bein' a little late, but Joe won't let a deer go to waste. He'll show up."

As L.D. finished his conversation with Bob, he wondered if Joe's reputation for promptness was facing some sort of serious trouble, and he admitted he was a little concerned. Although the wind was taken out of his fishing sails, L.D. knew he couldn't disappoint Stan by abandoning a sunny afternoon behind a rod and reel. So the two of them headed off to the pond that was 150 yards beyond the big red barn.

As they left, Bob said, "Check back with me before you leave for home. I'll probably have some news about Joe. If he needs some help with one of those record-book bucks you all say are in these woods, I'll come out back and give you a yell."

"Will do, Bob," L.D. responded. "And thanks again for the use of your pond."

Stan added, "Me, too, Mr. Gleason. Sure is nice to be out here today. I'll catch a big one for you!"

Joe noticed his hand was shaking as he looked down to check the position of his finger tab on the bow string. To help steady his nerves, he squeezed the nock of the arrow with the inside of his index and middle fingers. As he did, he realized he was yet to complete a ritual he invariably followed when his hunts began each morning. He always liked to get seated, then pull his bow to full draw to check for any unusual problems, such as sight pins that may have fallen out of position or sounds that might have developed that would spook a deer. As a result of his careful planning, it had been a long time since he'd had a problem in the moment of truth when a deer was coming into shooting range. He wanted desperately to complete the same ritual as he watched the creek bed, but he knew it was too late to be moving around and risk detection by the approaching gunmen. He would have to trust that his spare bow had remained in good working order, even after several days under his truck seat. His confidence level was not as high as he would have liked it to be. He quietly whispered a prayer, "Lord, You know I don't want to shoot at someone, but if I have to, help me do it right!"

Shelby found the creek bed and followed the edge of it, stepping as carefully as possible in the soft grass that lined the stream. He came to the spot where Joe had dropped out of the cedar thicket just minutes before. He started to step between a young maple tree and a large oak, and as he did, he encountered a low hanging spider web. It was a masterpiece of evil proportions. Shelby's face was covered with the micro-thin silver threads. He immediately began sputtering and wiping his face with disgusted vigor.

Joe heard the commotion and knew his assailant was only a few yards downstream. His heart raced with fear.

Shelby decided it would be safer to walk in the creek where it seemed to be void of the spider traps. When he stepped in, he gasped as the cold water suddenly soaked through his right tennis shoe. He stood there for a moment to try to get used to the icy pool. As he looked up and down the creek, his eyes fell on a brown, swirling trail of mud that drifted toward his feet on top of the water. Unknowingly, Joe had stirred up the silt on the floor of the creek. Unfortunately, it didn't go unnoticed. Shelby's eyes bugged as he realized how close he must have been to his target. He started to yell for Jack, but avoided the noise. Instead, he decided to go solo after the man and the truck keys they wanted so badly.

Holding his heavy pistol in both hands, with his right index finger on the trigger and both arms straight out at shoulder level, Shelby took slow, deliberate steps. He moved his arms in a wide, sweeping fashion, pointing the gun to one side of the creek and then to the other.

By then, Jack had worked his way to a vantage point where he could look down and see Shelby sneaking up through the water around the rocks and fallen tree trunks that lay along the banks. He could tell his partner was on to something. He dropped to one knee and anxiously observed Shelby's actions. Jack licked his lips in anticipation. Their chase would soon be over.

Lance Wilson backed out of his driveway, and sped off down the street. He radioed headquarters, "This is car 5 to central."

"10-4, car 5, this is central."

"I'm leaving my residence, Carla. Have you heard anything from the Tanners?"

"Negative, Wilson."

"10-4. I'd like to get clearance to run out to the Gleason farm. Could you do that for me?"

"Will do," she answered. "I'll get right back to you."

As Wilson waited for Carla's response to his request, he decided to call Evelyn as he'd promised. He picked up his phone and punched in the number. "Hello, Evelyn. This is Trooper Wilson again. Have you heard from your deer hunter yet?"

"No," came her soft but worried response.

"Well, I'm headed out to the Gleason place even as we speak." He knew he was offering her hope without first receiving permission from central to divert his duties to the other side of the county. However, he couldn't stand the thought of not being able to give Evelyn the comfort of knowing that someone was helping her put legs on her concerns.

As he turned onto Main Street and headed toward Bob's neck of the woods, he was relieved when the radio delivered the announcement, "Base to Wilson, you have a go to the Gleason farm."

"Excuse me, Evelyn, I need to respond to a call for a moment." Wilson put his phone on the dash, reached for his mic, and acknowledged Carla's announcement.

"10-4, Carla. I'm on the line now with Mrs. Tanner. I'll inform her that she can call you if she needs to contact me."

Wilson returned to the phone. "Evelyn?"

She answered, "I heard, and I'm so grateful for your help. I'll call your station if I need to get in touch with you. But, please, keep me posted on anything you find out, will you? I'm telling you, something is not right!" Evelyn continued with the question she was afraid to ask: "Have you heard any more about where those two fellows went who shot Mr. Simpson last night?"

Wilson wished he could offer Evelyn some good news. "No, I haven't. We're following every lead, and so far, none of them have taken us to the west end of the county, so don't let that concern you."

"I'll try not to, Lance. Thank you so much for calling." Her eyes turned to the clock on her microwave. Joe was now three hours late in coming home.

9

Evelyn pushed the off button on her phone after saying goodbye to Lance, but she didn't put it down. She dialed Bill Foster's number, hoping he was home and had heard from Joe.

"Hello," came a sweet female voice on the other end.

"Is this Shelly?"

"Yes, ma'am."

"Hi, Shelly. This is Evelyn Tanner. How's homeschooling?"

"Really fine. I didn't think I would like it, but it's great! Mom's a good teacher. She makes it fun."

"That's great, Shelly," Evelyn said. "Is your dad home?"

"No, he's still at work. Mama's here. I'll get her for you. Hold on."

As Shelly went to get her mother, Evelyn felt troubled. She wanted to strike out for the Gleason farm, but their three teenagers would be coming home soon. "Besides," she argued with her intuition, "this is probably one of those times I'll get to hear Joe apologize over and over again."

"Hello, Evelyn, this is Donna. It's so nice to hear from you. What's goin' on at the Tanner place today?"

"Well, I don't know if I should be worrying yet or not, but I'm concerned about Joe."

"Why? Is he sick?" Donna quickly asked.

"No, but I think I'd feel better right now if he were. He went hunting this morning out at the Gleason farm. He told me he'd be back by eleven, but he's not home yet, and I was wondering if you or Bill had heard from him."

"Evelyn, it's only two o'clock. You know those guys. They…" Donna stopped in midsentence and paused as she reconsidered her thoughts. "Well, I do have to say that Joe is a rare one. You know how Bill and L.D. are always kidding him about how bad he makes them look in the 'considerate husband' department. I know Joe would rarely make you wonder where he is. I've just kind of given up on Bill. If he comes home alive, I'm happy!"

"I know it's probably silly to be so concerned right now, Donna, but I have a feeling something isn't right." Evelyn hesitated. "And I'm sure you're aware of what happened last night at Harper's Store. Those two guys escaped, you know! I talked to Lance Wilson, and he confirmed it. At least they were headed in the opposite direction from the Gleason place—but you never really know."

Donna felt uneasy. "I talked with Bill around noon about the incident, and he seemed to think they probably left the area. He told me to keep our doors locked and curtains pulled just in case. There are a lot of backroads around this county. They could've circled and gone about any direction. How's that for comforting a friend?"

"That's okay, Donna. You're absolutely right about the roads in Giles County. I've been up and down them with Joe looking at field edges for deer. He has a real gift for making me believe we're going on a romantic evening drive through the country. He always has a gleam in his eye as we slowly creep along those back roads, but I'm no dummy. I know the word *dear* is spelled two different ways!"

"Bill should be home from work a little early today. As soon as he comes in, I'll see if he knows anything or has heard from Joe. Keep me posted, Evelyn. I'll also pray about this. I appreciate you letting me know what's going on."

Evelyn said goodbye and hung up the phone. As she did, she realized that in all the energy she was expending to fret over Joe, she'd

forgotten to talk to God about it. She leaned against the island counter in her kitchen and stared worriedly out the window into her backyard. She could see Joe's 3D deer target standing next to the fence in
front of a tall stack of hay bales. After a long sigh, she whispered a very
timely prayer for her husband that reverberated in heaven.

Jack decided to stay where he was and watch Shelby as he slowly
walked up the creek. He nervously chewed on his lower lip. "He's on
to something down there. We're about to get our man!"

Joe's body and mind were dealing with emotions he'd never known
before. He was realizing that being the hunter required concentration in terms of using his ears and eyes, but being the hunted yielded
an entirely different level of intensity. Never had his sight and hearing
been so focused. Like an old whitetail buck that bristles at the slightest
unusual sound or movement and crouches in readiness to run, every
fiber of Joe's being was on full alert.

He knew without a doubt that the hunter in the creek bed was
moving his way. Suddenly, through a small opening in the mass of
leaves and limbs that separated him from Shelby, Joe saw movement.
He froze solid as ice on the outside, but he was melting with fear on
the inside. He wondered how long he could keep his entire body from
quivering under the stress of the ordeal.

The gunman was a mere 30 yards away and pointing the six-inch
barrel of his pistol into the brush on the other side of the creek. Then,
as he took the next watery step, with stiffened arms he swung the gun
around and looked straight at the spot where Joe was crouched in the
tangled thicket. All Joe could do was silently scream, *God! Help me!* He
also prayed that his camo would blend with the foliage and deceive his
pursuer. He could see Shelby's eyes. They were wild and excited, like a
ravenous wolf would look at a weaker animal. For a moment, which
seemed like a week to Joe, Shelby stared into the brush in his direction,
then slowly turned his head to the opposite side of the creek. His arms
and the small cannon he held in his hands followed. As the pair of devi-
ant eyes turned away, Joe felt his body relax like a large, slowly deflating
balloon. He let out a sigh of needed relief. He knew the untrained eyes

of his enemy had not detected his presence. He now had an advantage. As Shelby was looking the other way, Joe cautiously rotated his head and checked the area above him on the hillside to see if the second man was moving. He was grateful that he saw nothing.

Once again, Shelby turned his gaze to Joe's position, moving his arms as he turned his head. It was as if he were covering his backside with his eyes, and his front side with his gun. It would be a method hard for Joe to defeat in terms of coming to full draw without being seen. He knew he'd have to do it when the gunman's head was turned away and before he moved his arms. He had to time it perfectly or the outcome would be disastrous. And the opening in the brush to shoot through was only about eight inches tall and four inches wide.

Use your 20-yard pin if you have to shoot, Joe reminded himself silently, wishing he could be anywhere but where he was. *Don't over-shoot; don't kill. Just disable him and run! Shoot for a leg or arm or shoulder. Don't kill the guy!* Joe couldn't believe what he was thinking.

Shelby looked right at the brush that held the husband and father of the Tanner household. Then his glance fell in front of him, about six feet away. In the middle of the creek, the water in a soggy impression that Joe's boot had made in the soft, black mud glistened in the sunlight filtering through the canopy of tall trees. With the look of a wolf about to pounce, Shelby scanned the brush ahead of him. It was as thick as fur, but he knew his target was somewhere close.

With the security of his .357 in hand, and assuming he held all the firepower, Shelby turned his head to the opposite side of the creek and began to swing his arms in the same direction.

Joe decided it was time. He pressed his shaking fingers onto the tightly mounted string on his bow and quickly came to full draw.

10

⋗⋅⋖⋗⋅⋄⋅⋖⋗⋅⋖

Joe's old compound bow was in good working order except for one small, dreaded problem that presented itself when he pulled the string back. In the two weeks it had been unused and in and out of the dry, warm conditions of the truck, it had developed a squeak in the lower wheel. Upon coming to full draw, the bow made a noise that sounded like someone stepping on a loose board in the floor of an old, empty house. The sound shot through the silent woods as if broadcast through a loudspeaker.

Shelby quickly turned, bent his knees in a policelike stance, and fired three rapid rounds into the brush in the direction of the noise. The spray of bullets was delivered about six to eight feet apart into the embankment. The blasts were unbelievably loud. Joe was stunned to the point that all he could think to do was remain at full draw, close his eyes, and wait for an impact somewhere on his body. As the roar of the gunfire settled, and Joe realized he was miraculously unharmed, he slowly moved his bow into position and put his white target pin on Shelby. Through his peep sight, Joe could see that the gunman was rebalancing himself from the recoil of the .357 and listening for signs of suffering in the brush. The seconds passed like hours as Joe held his ground at full draw.

With no audible indications that a bullet had found flesh, Shelby cautiously and slowly lowered his pistol to waist level. Once again he felt vulnerable standing in the stream with no one to watch his back, so he turned to check the opposite side of the creek. When he did, Joe took the needed opportunity to rest his arms that had begun to weaken under the 62 pounds of pull his old bow required. With as much strength as it took to get to full draw, he had to use the same amount to let the string down. Joe was grateful that the wheels turned silently and his muscles were getting a break. Though he had relaxed his draw, he wisely did not lower his bow to his side in case the enemy wasn't satisfied that the brush didn't conceal the hunter-turned-prey.

Once again, Shelby looked toward Joe's hiding place and assessed the area as the blue smoke from his .357 drifted slowly back down the creek. Then, without any warning that he was going to do it, Shelby angrily raised his pistol and fired three more rounds toward Joe. First, the leaves and dirt exploded three feet left of his position. Then, two feet to his right, the ground swelled under the impact of the second bullet. The third shot zinged over his head and tore into the trunk of an oak tree behind and above him.

Joe's ears rang with pain as he fought with everything in him to maintain his composure. He realized two things at once. One, he was still untouched by the destructive contents of the pistol, and two, the gun was out of bullets. Then, from down the creek he heard a voice that sounded muffled because his ears hadn't recovered from the sonic intrusion of the tremendous gun blasts they had just endured.

"Did you get him, Shelby?"

Joe made a mental note of the name and continued to watch his enemy.

Shelby looked in Jack's direction and, at the same time, began digging through his coat pockets for more ammunition. He retrieved six more rounds and began loading them into the cylinder. He responded with disgust, "Shut up, Jack! I know he's in there!"

Joe took note of the second name. He also saw that his pursuer was about halfway through his reloading process, and it required his eyes to get the job done. While Shelby was looking down at his weapon, Joe quickly came to full draw. The old bow had healed itself and operated with whisper-quiet cooperation. Joe suddenly found himself staring once again through his peep sight at the form of a man. Convinced it was a matter of self-defense and knowing the field-tipped arrow would not likely yield a fatal blow, he aimed for the fleshy, bulky part of the large brown leather coat that covered Shelby's right shoulder. He knew the impact could at least knock him off balance and give him a chance to run up the hillside and escape back into the cedar thicket.

Shelby looked over his shoulder again to check behind him and simultaneously pointed his gun toward Joe. Then he turned his eyes forward and squinted into the thick foliage. His facial expression revealed a depraved confidence that he knew right where his victim was hiding.

Joe silently whispered, *Don't do it, Shelby! Give it up. I don't want to take this shot!* He winced as the gunman's name echoed in his mind. It was a disturbing reminder that his target was human.

Too many seconds were passing for Joe to continue to hold at full draw without beginning to shake under the pressure the poundage was putting on his already tense muscles.

Then, as if preparing to fire at a range target, Shelby cupped the revolver in his sweaty hands and took careful aim into the underbrush. When he put his right thumb on the hammer, Joe decided to wait no longer. With the small, bright-white pin on a dark spot of Shelby's coat, and still unable to believe what was about to happen, he relaxed his fingers and allowed the string to slide over the smooth, black cow hair on the finger tab. The bow recoiled. As if in slow motion, Joe watched the neon green and white fletching as it passed through the small window in the brush and flew to its destination.

The arrow hit the leather coat with a soft thud and slid into Shelby's upper body. In the same instant, the .357 fired, flew out of his hand, and landed in two inches of water near the creek bank. Shelby staggered to his right and fell into the cold stream. The field-tipped arrow had penetrated his coat sleeve just below his armpit, slicing through the fleshy part of the inside of his upper arm. The fugitive was so shocked and surprised by the impact that he screamed in fear, "What was that? Jack, help me!"

Jack saw Shelby fall into the creek and heard him yell for his help. Too far away to clearly hear the snap of the bow limbs when Joe took his shot, Jack wondered what had caused his friend to suddenly fall. He descended the hillside quickly and ran toward his groaning partner, who was crawling through the shallow water toward the submerged pistol. Out of the corner of his eye, Shelby saw Jack running up the creek bed, and for a moment he abandoned his search for his weapon and looked at him with a bewildered gaze.

In the chaos created by his shot, Joe took the opportunity to sneak undetected up the hillside through the thickness of the underbrush. For a brief but valuable amount of time he was forgotten by the two men who were noisily meeting in the creek behind him.

Bill Foster pulled into his driveway at three o'clock, and Donna walked outside onto the porch of their Cape Cod-style home to meet her husband as she wiped her hands on an apron.

"Hey, sweetheart! How's my fav-o-rite lady today?" Bill greeted her as he had done nearly every day for 19 years.

"I'm fine, honey, but Evelyn's not doin' so well right now."

Bill was taken aback by the abruptness of Donna's announcement. "What's happenin' with Evelyn? Is she okay?"

"Well, it's not really her; it's Joe she's worried about. He went out to Bob Gleason's place this morning to bow hunt. He promised her he'd be home at 11 o'clock, and as far as I know he's not home yet."

"And let me guess…he hasn't called either. I know Joe Tanner well enough to know that he'd leave the treestand with a *Pope & Young Record Book* buck standing under him to make a phone call home before he'd let Evelyn and his family worry about him. It's not like Joe to forget to check in."

"Yes, I know that, sweetheart!" Donna responded, then suggested, "Maybe you should call Evelyn and see if she's heard anything. I'll warm up some of the spaghetti on the stove. Oh…have you heard any more about those two thugs who showed up in Grandville last night? Have they caught them yet?"

"As far as I know, they're still on the run, babe. The cops continue to search the east side of the county. That's where they were last seen. I also heard that a truck was stolen somewhere in that area." Bill started loosening his tie as he walked up the front steps.

As the two of them enjoyed a comforting embrace, Donna thought of Evelyn's serious concern for her man. "I sure hope those two guys are not anywhere near the Gleasons. Not only did Joe go out there this morning, but L.D. and Stan went out there this afternoon to fish. Evelyn said she had talked to Bob earlier, and he hadn't seen Joe today at all."

"Well, if necessary, I'm more than willing to cancel my lawn-mowing chore if my call to Evelyn doesn't bear good news about Joe's whereabouts." As Bill considered the possibility of serious trouble brewing among his friends, he forgot all about his appetite.

11

When Jack reached his wounded friend, Shelby moaned, "What was that? What in the world was it, Jack?"

Seeing the multishades of brown on the aluminum arrow that protruded from the back side of Shelby's coat, Jack said, "Well, ole buddy, I think you just had an encounter with Robin Hood. I thought I got rid of his bow, but he must've had another one somewhere in his truck!"

Then Jack looked around the woods nervously and offered Shelby a chilling thought. "He may have one of us in his sights at this very minute. He's so hard to see with that camo on. There's no tellin' where he is. But I'll say this, we can't let him get away. Not only has he seen our faces, after all this yelling we've done up and down the creek bed he probably knows our names!"

Jack looked down at Shelby, then he looked toward the brush where Joe had been hiding. "You were facing that side of the creek when you went down, weren't you?"

"Yes, but at the moment I don't want to think about that. I need some help here. I gotta get this thing out of my arm!"

Trying to avoid getting more wet than he had to, Jack bent over and grabbed the arrow near the field tip, and quickly tried to pull it on through Shelby's coat and the throbbing flesh under his arm.

Shelby screamed in pain. "Oh, man! Take it easy!" Jack had over-looked the fletching that prevented the shaft from being drawn through the wound, making the attempt twice as painful. He put his hand around the three, four-inch long plastic vanes on the opposite end and slipped the arrow out of Shelby's arm. "Sorry. Let's get your coat off and see what damage this thing did to your pitiful little body."

"You're about as funny as a cigarette in a cancer ward, Jack. Help me up."

Shelby removed his coat and shirt and was relieved to discover that the stinging wound was not life-threatening. "I guess goin' to a doctor is out of the question, but I gotta get somethin' to treat this hole in my arm. First chance we get, we gotta find a drugstore. I don't want to die of some sort of infection!"

"Good grief, Shelby," Jack said with little pity for his partner, "you're not gonna die. I've had worse injuries gettin' outta bed. Just be glad that arrow didn't have one of those razor blade-type points on it. You'd really be in a mess. Anyway, I have a feelin' that if that guy wanted to drill you in the heart, he probably could've easily done it. Now put your coat on and let's go find that man! We'd better hurry."

Shelby slipped on his coat, picked up his gun, and held his arm. He groaned as the muddy water continued to drip from his pants and coat. An intense anger welled up inside him. "Jack, I want that fool. I have a score to settle with him. Whatever we do, we can't let this guy get away from us!"

L.D. and Stan looked at each other across the pond when the sound of gunshots echoed in the distance. Nothing was said until finally Stan broke the silence of the peaceful environment. "Sounds like somebody is sightin' in their gun, gettin' ready for deer season, huh, Dad?"

"Yep," L.D. responded, while throwing his hook and sinker to the middle of the dark-green water, "except that gun didn't sound like a high-powered rifle to me. It sounded a little different. The shots were really close together. Whoever's doin' the shootin' is faster than ole Chuck Conners on *The Rifleman.*"

"Who's that, Dad?" Stan asked his father.

"Well, Stan, many years ago there was a TV show called *The Rifle-man*, and Chuck Connors played a character who could fire a lever-action rifle faster than lightning. He had a young son who was always involved in his dad's struggles to maintain peace in their little town. It was a great show."

"Is it in reruns?"

"I suppose it is, but I haven't seen that show in a long time. We should watch a few episodes together. I think you'd enjoy it. And by the way, little buddy, your bobber's gone!"

At that news, Stan looked at the ripples around his dancing red-and-white bobber and set the hook on a nice-sized bluegill. He began retrieving it as his dad thought further about the gunshots they had heard several minutes before. While Stan was taking the hook out of the quarter-pound brim, L.D. spoke up.

"You know, Stan, if that person was sightin' in a rifle, they sure got the job done quick. It usually takes me at least a half box of shells to do that chore. They must be good at it, or..." L.D. continued with an inquisitive voice, "maybe they're huntin'?"

Suddenly L.D. was overtaken by a curious thought that passed through his head, and he quickly said, "Stan, I hate to bring a good time to a screeching halt, but what say we take a drive around to where those shots came from and see what we can see?"

"Fine with me, Dad, but why?"

"Well, do you remember Bob sayin' something about Joe not showin' up at home on time, and how Evelyn was worried about him?"

"Yes."

"I just want to make sure I'm not missing something here. I want to drive around and see if his truck is still there. I know where he likes to enter the woods. If his truck is gone, then we can assume he's headed home and everything is probably okay." L.D. didn't add his worried thoughts about the recent gunshots and the two culprits who had shocked Grandville the night before.

"Well, let's do it," Stan said with a spirit of youthful adventure.

On the walk back around the barn to the big house, L.D. considered leaving Stan with Bob. However, he knew that if a search for Joe was necessary, extra eyes would be useful. Also, the thought of leaving his young son and an older gentleman alone without knowing whether the criminals were in the area was too unsettling.

Bob was surprised to see L.D. and Stan back so soon. "Well, guys, you're missin' the primetime in the fish kingdom. They're just now startin' to talk about their supper!"

"Yep, we know, Bob, but did you hear the gunfire over on the west side of your property?"

"No, I sure didn't. I've been downstairs workin' on a floor fan. I had the radio on, and I haven't heard a thing for the last hour except some jabbering on a talk show. I just came up to take a break."

"Well, Stan and I want to drive around and check it out and also see if Joe's truck is still there. We just want to be sure. We'd hate to miss something we should know. Want to come along?"

"I don't have anything else to do that can't wait," Bob said with a mature sense of cautious adventure. "Let me lock up and grab a jacket. I'll be right with you."

Joe was winded when he reached the crest of the hill. He had crawled and duck-walked his way for several minutes through the thick brush. Fortunately, he was able to avoid most of the briars, so the noise level of his escape was minimal. He rested on his knees to catch his breath. "I can't believe this. I just plugged a human being. I'm being hunted like an animal. I've been shot at, my truck won't start, and my nice buck is rotting. Could it possibly get any worse?"

Jack lowered his right hand into the creek and waved it around in the water to wash off Shelby's blood that had rubbed onto him when he was pulling out the arrow. He lowered his voice to a whisper as he looked toward Joe's recent hiding place.

"Now, you said you were facing that direction when you went down. I'm gonna go a little further up the creek and head up the hillside. You go down the other way and sneak up through those open woods. Find a good spot to hide. I don't think you want to get into that thicket there, not in your condition. I'll walk through that stuff and see if I can scare him. If he comes out, shoot him—and don't miss. And don't shoot me, whatever you do!"

Shelby started to walk away, but then he stopped. "I know we've got a lot more bullets than he has arrows. One of us has got to get this guy, Jack, and I hope it's me! I want him!"

"Yeah, you want *him*, but I want his *keys*!" Jack said with an irritated rage. "We both have good reasons to not give up. I don't think there's anybody else around to keep us from doin' what we gotta do. Let's be done with it. This little war won't last long!"

Joe could faintly hear the crunching of dry leaves below his new position as Jack and Shelby began to move. He strained to hear the sounds of footsteps above the singing birds and other noises that filled the woods. *Sounds like they've split up again,* Joe thought. The muffled crackling on the forest floor widened below him. Knowing the thicket ended about 100 yards ahead, Joe decided to position himself farther down the ridge and wait for a few minutes.

Jack headed up the hill, away from the creek about 200 yards, turned right, and entered the tight stand of cedars with his .357 in front of his chest, ready to fire at whatever moved. He stepped over, around, and through more foliage than he ever knew existed. He could not keep from making noise, and his anger was swelling as the sweat poured off his face.

"Man, this is ridiculous. We'll never find him in here." Little did he know that by the time he had worked through to the other side of the thicket and had come into view of Shelby, he had passed within 40 yards of Joe.

Shelby stepped out from behind the trunk of the red oak he was hiding behind and walked over to Jack and spoke quietly. "Well, that worked like a charm!"

"Give me a break, Shelby. You got any better ideas?"

"Hey," Shelby reminded Jack once again with indignation, "we wouldn't be in this mess if your friend would've showed up like he said he would! Why don't we head back to that bridge, get the money, and find another way out of here? You know the cops are gonna find that old coot we left for dead when we took his rattletrap of a truck last night. If that old clunker hadn't acted like it was gonna break down on us, we'd be well out of this territory by now."

Jack flailed his hand at a mosquito that flew around his face and looked around the woods. "I didn't think that old fellow would put up a fight like he did. And who would've known we'd be steered to a piece of junk that had 'farm use' painted all over the side of it?"

"I have a feeling he's in that mess you just came through, Jack," Shelby whispered. "Let's go through it together this time. I'm feeling okay enough to get this scumbag. I still want him awfully bad!"

"Yeah, I bet you do," Jack said, as he looked at the hole in Shelby's coat and smugly laughed.

About 80 yards away and hidden effectively, Joe laid prostrate in the leaves and looked underneath the brush trying to see the form of the man who had fought his way through the thicket behind him. Through one little opening, about three inches wide, he got a glimpse of not one, but two figures walking back toward the long, narrow undergrowth. Assuming they were not abandoning their attempt to find him, Joe decided that while they were preoccupied in the thicket, he would work his way through the open woods, head to the gravel road, and run like a rabbit south to Highway 12, about a mile and a half away.

As his pursuers made their move back toward the dense brush, Joe waited for the right moment to begin a quiet crawl toward the road. His heart pounded with excitement at the thought of successfully getting away from the two criminals. At that instant, from below him, he heard the sound of gravel under the tires of someone's vehicle as it slowly rolled up the road.

At the very same moment, Jack stopped in his tracks and excitedly yelled to Shelby, "Stop! Listen! Do you hear that?"

12

L.D.'s red Chevy pickup rumbled up the hill with a low but powerful roar. As it slowly neared the point directly below Joe's position, L.D. looked at the multishades of early autumn colors in the dense hillside. "Bob, you sure do have a beautiful place here!"

"Well, thank you…and I have to agree. Truth is, though, I haven't seen much of the world beyond this place, not that I need…or…even want to, of course."

For a moment L.D. studied the careful way Bob said his words. Then, with keen discernment, he spoke to the heart of his elderly friend. "Sounds to me like you've been thinkin' about that lately. Are you feelin' some regrets, Bob?"

Bob looked somewhat surprised. "How'd you figure that out, L.D.? I thought I could slip that one by. Sarah always said my skull was made of glass and that she could always see right through my head and could read what my brain was thinking. I guess you have that ability, too."

"Naw, it's not that, Bob," L.D. commented as he rolled his window down, put his elbow out, and rested his arm on the door. "It's the old 'out of the abundance of the heart, the mouth speaketh' thing. I've found if you listen close, you'll hear what a person is really feeling."

"I just wish I would've taken Sarah a few places in her day. She always wanted to go to the Holy Land. I couldn't convince her that we lived on 'em!"

"I agree with you, Bob. There's a peace on this property unlike I've seen anywhere else in my time. I believe you and Sarah must've baptized this place with prayers. There just seems to be a heavenly protection here. I've always wanted to mention that to you. I also want to tell you how grateful and honored I am to be able to walk in these hills."

Bob nodded thanks for L.D.'s compliment. "We just didn't have a lot of adventure as a couple, and it was really my fault. Every day was filled with the cares of life until finally we got too old to think about travelin'...at least that's what I thought. I sure wish I would've done some of it with her now." Bob paused and looked out the window toward the hillside and sighed. "But she made a journey that topped them all. Where she is...it's a far better place. I sure look forward to seein' her again."

"Me, too, Bob. I believe *we will see her again* someday. And truth is, a fellow never knows when that day will come. It pays to be ready!"

Bob nodded his head in agreement. "Amen!"

Evelyn's phone rang and she quickly picked it up. With hopeful anticipation, she answered, "Hello!"

"Evelyn, it's Bill. Donna told me about your concern for Joe. Have you heard anything yet?"

"Oh, Bill, I haven't heard anything, and I'm starting to get *really* worried. Joe wouldn't leave me wondering about him this long."

"You're right about that," Bill admitted.

Evelyn recalled an incident that added to her anxiety. "You probably remember our former neighbor's fall out of his treestand a few years ago. He nearly killed himself. The same thing could've happened to Joe. He may be out there laying in a heap, unable to move." Evelyn hesitated. "And with those two gunmen still on the loose..."

"I can see how you could feel that way, Evelyn. But let's consider the possibilities. His truck could've broken down. Sometimes it's the brand-new vehicles that give us the most headaches. Or it's possible

that he's got a deer down, and for once in his life, he's actin' like the rest
of us numbskulls. He could very well be involved with a blood trail!"

"True," Evelyn agreed, "but he's got his phone with him, and I know
it's charged. He plugged it in last night, and it wasn't here when I got up.
It's just not like him to not let me know something…and it's 3:30 now!"

"You've got a point, Evelyn," Bill conceded, and then he offered his
help. "I believe I'll drive out to Bob's and see if there's any word yet. I'm
sure Joe wouldn't want you to be going through this worry. Try not to
let the old imagination factory run too long. Let's trust God that everything's gonna turn out all right."

"I'll do my best, Bill, and thank you for your help. By the way, in
case you didn't know, L.D. and Stan went out there to fish this afternoon. Lance Wilson took his patrol car out there to check around,
too. Joe will probably be embarrassed if the whole town shows up out
there! I'll stay here and tend to the phone, serving as a check-in point
for everyone. I'll keep my conversations short in case you try to call."

"I'll have my phone, too. Do you have my number?"

"Sure do. I have it right here on my bulletin board. Bless you, Bill."

"Thanks, Evelyn, and we'll be prayin'."

Joe was fighting the urge to break into a noisy run toward the vehicle that was moving up the road below him. In the very same moment,
at the end of the Currey River Bridge about two miles away, a man in
an older model, white, 4x4 Chevy slapped his steering wheel in disgust
and then started his engine. As he let it idle, his voice filled the cab with
a speech that was heard by only his own ears.

"This is my fourth trip to this stupid bridge in less than 24 hours.
That idiot Jack Brewer! I knew he was trouble from the start! But he
knows too much about my past to cross him now. After I get through
this episode with that imbecile, I guess I'll have to leave this area and
start all over somewhere else!"

With both hands in a death grip on the steering wheel, angrily pulling it back and forth as if he were trying to rip it out of the dash, the
man continued his complaining. "That idiot's messin' up a great situation here! I love this place, and now I've got to give it up for some

two-bit convict. I oughta call the cops right now and turn him and his buddy in. Man, everybody here accepts me. I like that."

Earl Potter ended his troubled assessment of his situation by staring stonily out the window. In the past he would have added a few choice words learned on the streets of Chicago years earlier. But in an effort to blend in with the locals, he had trained himself to avoid using profanity, knowing it would not set well with the respectable folks he had come to know in rural Giles County. He was pleased with an accomplishment that had required some serious self-discipline. Earl had done well in his atempt at decency...until Jack Brewer phoned him around 8 o'clock the previous evening. The call came nearly two hours after he and Shelby had robbed Harper's Grocery and critically wounded Phillip Simpson. Earl seethed as he recalled hearing Jack's opening words when he answered the phone the night before.

"Hey, Tony, how's it goin' with my old friend?"

When the caller addressed him by his real name, one he had long forsaken, Earl knew the person was from somewhere in his past.

The caller continued. "Hey, man, it's Jack Brewer. You know...the former Mrs. Jack Brewer's husband. It's your favorite ex-brother-in-law!"

Earl's heart dropped when he realized who he was talking to. The man was the last person on earth he wanted to hear from again. Before his sister had finally gained a divorce, Jack had learned too much about Earl's role as a key player in a ring of heroin and cocaine dealers in Chicago. In an attempt to rid himself of his worthless brother-in-law, Earl tipped the police concerning the location of one of Jack's planned drug deals, and the resulting incarceration brought an immediate retaliation. Earl's "business" associates suddenly started receiving visits from the Chicago police department, and the heat was on. He quickly fled from the city to look for a safe haven and settled in the first place that seemed friendly to a stranger. He eventually became known to a few folks around the county as "the city slicker turned farmer."

Earl Potter, formerly Tony Manzana, had managed to slide out of his past like a snake shedding its skin. He bought false identification, changed his hairstyle, got a "real job" with a construction company, and forced himself to enjoy blue jeans in an effort to disappear into the simplicity of life in the Currey River Valley. He knew the return of an old nemesis, especially in the form of Jack Brewer, would spoil his cover. His anger grew as he thought about it.

"How did you get my number?" Earl had quickly demanded, bypassing any formal greetings.

"Hey, Tony! You have family that I used to hang around with at one time. Remember? They knew enough about you that I was able to put the pieces together, and here I am! Now that I've found you—and it wasn't easy to do—I thought you'd like to know that I have lots of numbers in the little black book I carry with me that represent a lot of people who'd like to talk to you. I haven't passed your new locale around to anybody yet, but I'd do it if I had to. Now, with that in mind, do you think you can help us out?"

With that threat, Earl suddenly felt sick to his stomach.

"What's the deal, Jack?" he asked quietly.

"Listen, my buddy Shelby and I were sent to this area on a little business, and we have a situation that came up. We had to pick up a few bucks for our expenses and some 'do-gooder' got in our way. We had to put the guy down, and now we've got the law after us. Our car quit, and we need your assistance, ole buddy. Knowing your history, I knew for sure you'd be happy to help us out!"

Earl's temper flared. "For the record, Jack, my history is just that—history! I'm not the guy you knew a few years ago. Keep that in mind. What do you want from me?" He was hoping that whatever was required would not put his life in a total uproar.

"Just help us get out of this predicament, and we'll leave you alone. You got any ideas?" Jack inquired while his eyes scanned the street from the phone booth where he and Shelby were huddled.

Earl quickly thought of ending the conversation by just hanging up. To do so would risk the inevitable damage of Jack's revenge. On the other hand, getting briefly involved with the pair might serve to salvage the comfort and security of the inconspicuous country life he had come to enjoy. Helping the two outlaws seemed less disruptive at that moment. "Where are you now, Jack?"

"We're near…" Jack paused to look around for a landmark, "a

store by the name of Jim's Quickmart. We're…" Jack stopped in mid-sentence. His voice suddenly rose with excitement. "Tony, I see a car coming down the road. We gotta hurry. Come up with something quick!"

"Okay, Jack. You need to get to the bridge that crosses over Currey River on Highway 12. That's about 18 miles west of Grandville, and it's the best route out of the county. If you'll look behind the market, you'll see a field. It's dark right now, I know, but it's just a level cornfield. Go across it and you'll see a house about a quarter mile back there. That's old man Scutter's place. I've done some work for him. I know he's got an old truck, and it usually sits out in his front yard. I bet he keeps the keys in it. They do that around here. Just promise me you'll leave him alone if the keys aren't there. Call me back, instead!"

Jack interrupted Earl's instructions. "My phone's almost dead." He paused. "My number is in your phone's memory now. Keep talkin'!"

"Just get the truck and head west on the hardtop in front of his house. Follow it for about five miles till you come to a 'T' in the road. Go right, and that'll lead you to an old dirt road that goes along the river. It's not the greatest, but it'll keep you away from any checkpoints that might be set up on the main highway."

Jack broke in again. "I'm followin' ya, keep goin'!"

"Just find your way to that bridge. I'll try to time it right and be there waiting for you. Look for a white Chevy 4x4. If you don't show up, I'll leave and come back. If you do make it, and I'm not there, park the truck below at the boat ramp, and wait under the bridge. I'll blow my horn twice when I come back. Just wait for me."

"You better be there, Tony!"

Earl recalled how much he detested Jack's intimidation, and worse, how much he hated to say, "I'll be there."

13

Earl checked the clock on the wall of his small kitchen. Eight o'clock. Hoping to give Jack enough time to make the unfamiliar drive, he decided to wait until 8:30 to go to the bridge. As he waited for the time to leave, he was surprised that the name Sarah Gleason came to mind. He'd tried to politely avoid her whenever he stopped by the Gleason farm. Her motherly invitations to stay for supper and her friendly smile had finally won his heart. He thought of how persistent she was that he should seriously consider where his soul would live in eternity.

Earl was puzzled by the emotions he felt as he poured a cold cup of coffee into a mug and placed it in the microwave that sat on a table next to the refrigerator. After thinking it through for a few minutes, it occurred to him that it was Sarah who represented the very reason he'd grown to love Giles County. She reminded him of his own mama. He also thought of the tender years with his mother that were sadly consumed by the "bad company" he'd chosen to associate with in the Windy City. How many times had she said with tears in her eyes, "Son, don't you know that bad company corrupts good morals?"

The truth of those words rang painfully clear in Earl's heart as he battled with the decision of whether to remove the .38-caliber revolver from the bottom of a heavy ceramic jar sitting on top of a kitchen cabinet. Frightened and struggling to admit that he was scared, he wished he could somehow call Sarah on the phone or call his mama and pour out his fears and beg them to pray. As he stared at the jar that held his pistol, he suddenly sensed that watching him from somewhere above were two women who would not agree with him leaving his house armed.

Earl surprised himself when he softly whispered, "Oh, God, help me!" The words came out amazingly unforced yet desperately sincere. He walked out of his kitchen without the revolver. Praying was uncharted territory for him since he'd never really experienced such debilitating fear before. What he did fear at that moment, however, was not physical harm. Instead, he shuddered at the thought of losing the peaceful existence that was free of having to wake up day after day worried about getting caught and living like a hunted animal. His past was a lifestyle he'd rather die than return to. As if speaking to someone who was standing next to him, he asked, "How can I continue to hide my worthless past and salvage my future? Will I ever find real peace?"

Finally, 8:30 came and Earl locked the door to his modest home where he had lived as a bachelor for the previous years. He nervously headed out for what would turn out to be the first of several trips to the bridge. For once, he was glad there was no one to say goodbye to as he walked off the small, concrete porch into the darkness and climbed into his Chevy. When he turned the key to start the motor, the radio came on and the local country station was broadcasting the news about the robbery, as well as the trail of tears that the bandits had left for the Simpson family. Earl knew he was stepping into a deep pool of trouble by offering his assistance to the two men he wished didn't exist. As he rolled out of his graveled driveway and onto the road that would lead him to Highway 12—and the Currey River Bridge—Earl was once again surprised by the idea that had come to him a little while earlier: "Pray!"

When he arrived at the bridge at 8:45, he drove across it, parked at the west end, turned off the motor, and sat in the dark silence. The minutes slowly passed as he watched the other end of the bridge for headlights. Finally, around 9:15, a set of low beams rounded the bend about a half-mile beyond the bridge. Earl's heart filled with gnawing regret. The lights drew closer and closer, and then passed on by. It was not Mr. Scutter's light-green truck. He called Jack's phone number, but there was no answer.

Assuming that Jack and Shelby had been delayed for some reason, Earl started the engine, put the Chevy in drive, slowly pulled away, and headed back toward his house. He could only guess how angry Jack would be if the rest of the night unfolded and they failed to connect.

Ten minutes after Earl left the quiet darkness that engulfed the bridge, another vehicle approached. It was Scutter's old truck, sputtering and clanging like a Model-T as Jack brought it to a brief stop on the east end of the bridge. Not seeing a white 4x4 anywhere around, Jack drove to the west end, and Shelby asked with a cynical jab, "Where's your so-called friend?"

Jack was agitated. "Well, between trying to find this old rattletrap of a truck and driving through the boonies in the dark, what did you expect? Looks like we'll have to wait here a while. But first we gotta get rid of this heap of junk!"

Jack and Shelby opened the squeaky doors of the old truck, got out, and walked to the side of the bridge. They looked down into the blackness below. Jack wheeled around and climbed into the driver's seat. "Get in, Shelby! Tony mentioned there's a boat ramp down there somewhere. Let's take this piece of junk down and launch it!"

They drove down to the river, put the pickup in gear, and jumped out of the cab. As the top of the old truck disappeared under the surface of the Currey River, Jack turned to Shelby and assessed their status. "We've gotta get out of this area. We're way too hot!"

"Well, we're out here in the middle of nowhere, our phones are dead, we just drowned our only ride, it's as dark as death, and your friend is nowhere to be seen. Does that sound like mother luck is smiling on us?"

"We've gotta find another way out. If daylight comes and Tony hasn't shown up, we'll just have to walk to one of those friendly farmer's houses around here so we can take from the poor and give to the rich!" Jack smiled and held up the tan-colored duffel bag that contained, among other things, two full-face ski masks and about $5500 in cash. "We'll find a way, Shelby. We'll get help one way or another."

"Didn't Tony say to get up under the bridge and wait?" Shelby asked.

Jack looked up at the jet-black darkness of the understructure of the old bridge and said, "Yes, and I'm sure it's a cozy place under there with the spiders...and who knows what else that would like to eat us for a midnight snack!"

Both of them climbed up the grassy bank and ducked their heads as they walked as far back under the bridge as possible. The concrete was cold as Shelby sat down. "It ain't no Hilton, but I'm tired enough that I think I could actually sleep under here. Wake me up when you hear the horn!"

Jack laid back for a moment on the cold, damp concrete. "This'll do. I can hear a car when it comes. I'm sure Tony will be here; he's got too much at stake. We just took too long to show up and missed him."

Jack sat up, then Shelby laid back and pulled the duffel bag under his head for a pillow. He closed his eyes, and in a few minutes he was sound asleep, snoring lightly with no apparent feelings of remorse or regret for the pain and loss he had inflicted on the people in Grandville just five hours earlier.

Jack looked down at the black water of the river and, for the first time since the robbery, contemplated the events of the evening. "I sure wish folks wouldn't get in my way. I hate it when they do that. I bet we're a hot topic of discussion in..." Jack couldn't immediately remember the name of the town. "Where were we? Oh, yes! Grandville!" As if the reality of the potential consequences of his actions suddenly dawned on him, he whispered, "They'll not take me alive. No way. I'm not goin' back to the slammer...ain't no way!"

Jack reached into his coat pocket and pulled out a Reese's Peanut Butter Cup he'd taken off the shelf as they were leaving Harper's Grocery. He'd been waiting for the chance to consume it without having to share it with Shelby. He put both discs of partially melted chocolate and peanut butter into his mouth and moaned with pleasure as he savored the only meal he'd enjoyed since they'd started their escapades earlier that evening.

Jack licked his fingers, then put his head back on the concrete wall which he sat against. About 30 minutes passed, and he stared into the night, dazed and tired to the very core of his being. As if in the grips of the "sugar blues," his eyes slowly closed and he began to lose the battle against the slumber that he tried hard to resist. He drifted off for a moment and then came to again. "I'd better wake up Shelby. I'm not doin' too good here. I'll let him sleep ten more minutes, then I'll trade places with him."

When 10 minutes had gone by, both of the men were out cold on the hard concrete floor of the bridge support. About 30 minutes later, around midnight, as they snored in harmony, Earl's headlights illuminated the entire length of the bridge for the second time that evening, and he sat with his motor running on the east end. Underneath the west end of the bridge, Jack and Shelby were unconsciously fighting to stay warm as they tossed and turned in the mid-60s temperature of the night. Earl tapped his horn twice in a set of very brief beeps; the high-mileage Chevy spoke in an unusually soft voice. The two men under the bridge never heard the signal. They slumbered through, totally unaware that Earl was once again pulling away and heading back to his house.

14

⊰⦿⊱

Finally the sun rose and the early light found the underside of the bridge. Jack's eyes fluttered open. When it dawned on him what a slumbering mistake he'd made, he bolted upright, looked around, and screamed, "Oh, man!" He grabbed Shelby by his coat that was pulled up over his head. "Bad news, buddy! We've overslept!"

Shelby moaned in pain as he put his hand on the cool, damp concrete and shoved himself into a sitting position. With the other hand he rubbed his unshaven face. "What do you mean, *we*? I don't remember being woke up to keep watch!"

Jack was exasperated for allowing daylight to come with the two of them still waiting under the bridge. "Where is Tony? Did you ever hear a horn, Shelby?"

"No! The last thing I heard was you promisin' to wake me up when you got tired. You must've passed out. Did you hear anything at all?"

Jack crawled out from the cavelike crevice where they had been hiding, stood fully upright, and stretched while holding his aching back. "I sat there for 30 or 45 minutes last night, and I didn't hear one car pass over this bridge, let alone a horn! I must've drifted off." Jack removed his cap, sighed deeply, and ran his cold, dirty hands through his hair. "Now that I think about it, I guess I did hear some traffic this morning, but I must've thought I was dreaming. Boy, I'm tired."

Shelby rolled his eyes in disbelief and looked down at the concrete that had tortured him through the night. He shook his head in disgust. "Well, it looks like it's pretty early. The fog would be gone by now if it were later in the morning. Let's go up and take a look around. Maybe there's a house nearby."

The two groaned as they fought the pain of having slept on the rock-hard surface and carefully climbed to the edge of the road. They looked west and saw only the deserted continuation of Highway 12. Jack looked east and pointed to the other side of the river. "Shelby, do you see that road down there, goin' off to the left, beyond the end of this bridge? That's the gravel road we finally reached and followed to this main highway last night. It forks about a quarter of a mile off the highway. I didn't see any houses on the road we came down. Maybe there's one on the other fork. We ought to try it."

Shelby agreed, then suggested, "Why don't we stash the duffel bag out of sight up under this bridge before we take a walk. We can come back and get it, and it isn't wise to carry this thing around. We'll go see if we can find a 'volunteer' to help us with transportation. It won't do us any good to stay here. I'm surprised that we didn't get a wake-up call by the 'badge' last night. They usually don't leave a stone unturned. Maybe we're too far out of town for them to check. But sooner or later, they'll show up."

Jack anxiously looked in both directions. "Maybe you're right. Let's see what we can find up that road. But let's be quick crossing this bridge. I don't want to jump into the river if we hear a car coming!"

With the duffel bag secured above a section of angle iron under the bridge, the two desperate partners quickly ran across the span without stopping until they were about 100 yards up the gravel road that went left off of Highway 12. At the "Y" in the road, they headed to the right. Once out of sight and sound of the main road, they unknowingly fell victim again to bad timing. Earl arrived at the bridge for the third time since the evening before and slowly drove across it. He tapped his horn, waited a few minutes, then drove away when no one responded to his call.

After nearly a half hour of walking and arguing about whether or not to turn around and go back to the highway, Jack decided he needed a break. "Let's stop here and rest a minute, Shelby. Maybe somebody'll drive by we can flag down."

"Sure, Jack." Shelby put his arms out wide and looked up and down the quiet road. "This is a regular interstate out here. Ain't nobody gonna drive by. Let's go back to the paved road."

"Use your head," Jack shot back. "After what we did yesterday evening, anyone who saw two guys walkin' down a deserted highway lookin' like we do would probably call the cops."

"Well, do you have any brighter ideas than actin' like Lewis and Clark out here in this wilderness? Our chances of gettin' away are lookin' mighty slim to me."

Jack sighed impatiently through tight lips. "Let's just rest, then we'll walk a little further up this road. We're bound to find somebody around these parts!"

For a longer time than they planned, the two sat on the bank that edged the road and discussed how they would explain their unplanned delay when reporting to the people who had hired them. After finally settling on a story they both felt was believable, Shelby vented his anger regarding their stop at Harper's Grocery.

"Jack, I wish you would've left well enough alone yesterday evening! We didn't really need that cash. We should've just made the drop at the bus station like we were hired to do and gone on back!"

"Hey, those people don't pay enough money for this kind of work. I did what I had to! Anyway, what are you complainin' about? You're gonna come out okay on this one, too!"

Finally, they decided to get moving again. As the morning slowly wore on, they rounded a turn in the road and surprised their first victim of the new day. It was a lone hunter struggling to hoist his heavy deer into his 4x4. The deadly game of hide and seek began.

Trooper Wilson turned left into the driveway of the Gleason home, parked, but left the motor running. He opened his door and, with some effort, wrestled his large frame out of the car. He walked up to the front door of the old house. Two sets of unanswered knocks convinced him that Bob wasn't home. Knowing the older gentleman lived alone, he walked to the rear of the house, checked the windows and back door, and generally sized up the place for any suspicious activity. After a complete trip around the huge structure, Wilson was satisfied that things were normal.

After waiting at the Gleason home for a while, Lance looked anxiously at his watch for the third time, then looked up at the afternoon sun. "Well, I guess it's time I head back to the station." With his large hands, he pushed his tall body away from the trunk lid that he had been leaning against. At that moment, the radio broke the silence.

"Central to car 5."

Wilson quickly reached through the open patrol car window and pulled the microphone outside. "10-4, Carla, this is 5."

"Wilson, a call just came in that you may be interested in."

"Uh…10-4, go ahead."

"Steve Young, who lives outside of Grandville, reported that he had seen a white sports utility vehicle parked at the west end of the Currey River Bridge last night around 9:15. He said he wouldn't have thought anything of it had it not been for all that took place here last night. You can check it out if you think it's important since you're in the area."

"10-4, Carla. I'm not too far from the bridge. I'll go over and take a look. I'm on my way."

As the October afternoon grew warmer, Jack and Shelby's pursuit of the hunter and his truck key had seriously heated up as well, especially after the one arrow had delivered a well-placed blow. The chase suddenly stalled when all three of them had heard the sound of the popping gravel under the tires of the vehicle on the road below. Someone was entering the danger area!

Joe could hear the two men blasting out of the thicket as they tore through the open forest toward his disabled truck, which was about 250 yards from them. Preoccupied with finding a new way out, neither Jack nor Shelby saw Joe even though they ran within 30 yards of him. Once they were well past and making enough noise to wake the dead, Joe took off in a straight line down the hill toward the road.

As he drew near he could see the form of the vehicle moving slowly along. Unable to identify it, he continued ahead, hoping to get to it before it passed him. He stopped for a second to listen. Jack and Shelby were still at a full run. With the road slightly more visible through the foliage, Joe could see that it was a red vehicle and his timing wasn't going to be good enough to intercept the driver.

As he came to the edge of the road he stopped in horror. It was a truck he recognized—L.D.'s old Chevy! Ironically, it had L.D.'s favorite bumper sticker on the tailgate: Real Success Is Ending Up in Heaven.

15

As the truck neared the slight curve in the road about 50 yards to his right, Joe searched his mind frantically for how to handle another impending crisis. Beyond the bend was his own pickup, and he knew very well that at any moment the two perpetrators would appear. He quickly stepped to the center of the road, out of sight of the place where Jack and Shelby would likely drop out of the woods. Trying not to alert them, Joe quietly, but vigorously, waved his bow above his head in a jumping jack motion to get L.D.'s attention.

The stoplights illuminated on the rear of the truck and Joe rejoiced. He waited anxiously for the white lights to come on indicating that L.D. was putting the truck in reverse. Without yelling, he gave the "come back here" signal with his free hand, but nothing happened. The truck seemed to be suspended in uncertainty.

Joe held his breath. Perhaps the truck's occupants hadn't seen him. He hoped L.D. would not proceed any farther. *He probably saw my truck and stopped.* He moved to the edge of the road and began to quickly walk toward L.D.'s pickup.

Suddenly, Jack and Shelby burst out of the woods in front of L.D. and immediately ran toward the red pickup. Joe quickly dashed to the bushes that lined the edge of the forest.

Two miles away, Lance Wilson's patrol car slowly moved across the long, flat concrete surface of the Currey River Bridge.

"Car 5 to central."

"Central to car 5, come back," Carla responded.

"I don't see any vehicle or person around the bridge. Anything else happening I need to know about?"

"No. What are your plans now?"

"I think I'll head back over to the Gleason place and check one more time to see if Bob's home yet. If not, I'll go back to town."

Wilson hung his radio mic back onto the dash bracket, turned around on the west end of the bridge, and headed east to the Mill Creek Road turnoff. He wasn't aware of the alternate route he could have taken to the Gleason farm across Six Mile Road, where trouble was brewing at the top of the hill. He also had no idea how close he was to the tan duffel bag hidden just below him.

Evelyn was fighting her fears with all the strength she could muster. Tears waited at the gates of her eyes as she looked at her watch: 3:45.

Matthew, their 16-year-old son, pleaded with his mother. "Mom, let's go look for Dad!"

"Matt, we can't risk being gone and your dad coming home or maybe a call coming in from someone else about his whereabouts."

Bessie, the 18 year old, spoke up. "Mom, why don't we go out to the Gleason place? We can't just sit around here and wait."

To divert her kids from talking her into doing something irrational, Evelyn said, "I agree this is difficult. Deep in my heart I feel he needs our help, but I'm just not sure that forming a family posse is a good thing to do. Make sure you all are praying about this situation. Your dad will show up sooner or later, and then we'll all box his ears!"

Stan quickly sat upright and pointed out the front window of the truck. "Look, Dad! Who are those two guys?"

Bob put his hand nervously on the dash. "Good grief, L.D., those men have guns!"

L.D. jerked his gearshift into reverse and spun the tires. As he accelerated, he excitedly announced, "That was Joe's new truck sitting there…and I'm afraid I know who those two men are who are running this way. We've got to get out of here!"

When L.D. turned his head to look out the back window of his truck in order to drive in reverse, he got a momentary glimpse of the form of a man, standing at the edge of the road. He quickly looked forward. "There's someone back there. You two get down—and quick! Bob, lock your door!"

In the chaos of the sudden crisis, L.D. didn't have time to wonder who the third person was behind him. As Bob lowered his head as far as he could, he searched for the old-fashioned lock button and pushed it downward. "Lock yours, too, L.D.!"

Stan could see that his dad was preoccupied with all that was taking place outside the truck, so he quickly reached across L.D.'s lap and locked his door. He then rolled the window up as fast as he could turn the crank handle.

Jack screamed at Shelby as he darted toward the truck. "Don't shoot it. We don't need another worthless ride! We'll need those wheels! Just get those people out of there!"

Jack looked at L.D. and yelled at him at the top of his lungs. "Stop the truck…or I'll blow you away!"

As he stepped on the accelerator, L.D. heard the command through the glass of his cab. Assuming the person behind the truck was an accomplice, he decided that if he continued he'd be looking down another gun barrel. He slid to a stop, and when he did, Jack and Shelby stopped in their tracks.

"That's right," Jack loudly called out. "Now get out of the truck!"

"Stay down, guys," L.D. instructed his passengers. "I'm gonna use my 'Chevy-.06' to get us out of here and go for help!"

At that statement, L.D. dropped the shifter into forward gear and mashed the gas pedal. Jack immediately opened fire. Of the three rounds that were spent, the first broke the front windshield and entered the seat just above Stan's left shoulder. Two inches lower, and Stan would be dead. The second shot grazed the roof, and the third zinged through the truck by L.D.'s head and shattered the entire rear window.

As the pieces of broken glass fell behind the seat, and into their laps, L.D. brought the truck to a standstill.

"I can't believe this is happening!" he cried.

"The next one goes in your head," Jack said as he approached the passenger's side. "Now get out of there, all three of you! You won't be needing this truck anymore today."

Bob reasoned with L.D. "I think we'd better do what the man says, ole buddy. These fellows obviously mean business!" As they unlocked their doors, they anxiously watched the two crazed men whose eyes were filled with rage.

Stan was visibly shaken as he slid across the vinyl seat and stepped outside of the truck behind Bob. L.D. reluctantly opened his door, and, with his hands partially in the air, he walked around to the passenger side and joined Stan and Bob. The three of them stood there bewildered, frightened, and nervous.

Jack maintained a policelike stance with his weapon just four feet in front of his three captives. "Shelby, come over here and take care of these three. Hurry up! Looks like the truck is still alive, and it's ours now!" Jack shouted.

Joe overheard Jack's orders and his emotions ran high as he wondered what Shelby was about to do. Concealed by the brush at the road's edge, he quietly moved to a position within sight of the crowd that was gathered 40 yards away.

Jack's back was to him, and Shelby was preoccupied with moving his three captives to the side of the road in front of the truck. "Get over here, turn around, and get on your knees. Do it now!"

L.D., Stan, and Bob were in total shock at the turn of events. As they followed the stranger's commands, L.D. wondered where—and who—the third person was he had seen behind the truck. It suddenly occurred to him who it must have been. *It has to be Joe. Otherwise, whoever it was would already be here to join in this mess!*

"What are you gonna do with us?" Stan asked with a weak voice.

"Just shut up, kid, and kneel down!"

L.D. spoke up, "Don't you think the gravel is a little hard on an old fellow's knees, mister?"

Shelby ignored L.D.'s appeal on Bob's behalf and angrily shouted to his captives, "Turn around, all of you, and kneel down!"

Bob's heart raced as he whispered a quick and very sincere prayer. "God, we're facing the devil himself. We need a miracle!"

"Don't do this, mister," L.D. pleaded. "Just take the truck and my wallet—it's got at least $75 in it. Just let us walk out of here!"

"What's your name?" Shelby asked, as Jack moved behind him and climbed into the wounded but working old truck.

"My name is L.D."

"Oh, so you're the friend of the jerk who nailed me back in the woods with one of his pitiful little arrows." Shelby ignored the pain that still ran down his arm from the shot Joe had made earlier.

"What?" L.D. asked, as he looked over his shoulder toward the area he had last seen Joe.

"Oh, never mind, and just keep quiet!"

Jack was getting really nervous. He cranked the window down and leaned his head out. "Hurry up, Shelby. That jerk you're talkin' about is probably gonna show up any minute. Do what you gotta do, and let's get out of here!"

Shelby flinched at the possibility of dealing with another hole in his body. He quickly glanced in all directions, then stood behind the three helpless captives who knelt with their backs to him on the edge of the road in the sharp gravel. He raised his gun. When Joe saw that his friends' lives appeared to be in grave danger, he quickly stood upright, came to full draw, and stepped out into the road.

Shelby deliberately pointed his gun. "You're first, old man!"

When Joe heard those deadly words, he found his 40-yard pin in his peep sight and placed it just above Shelby's upper left arm. Joe said another prayer of guidance for the arrow and let the string slide across the tab that protected his fingers.

16

~·―◄►·―O―◄►·―◄

The shot from the compound bow made a familiar sound in L.D.'s ears. He'd never been on the target end of an arrow in flight. In the last few feet of its approach, he could actually hear the fletching as it cut through the wind, making a light whooshing sound. Knowing that the target stood right behind him, he took comfort only in Joe's excellent skill as an archer.

Shelby also heard the snap of the bow limbs, and although he was newly acquainted with the sound, he didn't have time to react. In the next instant, an arrow passed through the meaty part of his left upper arm, just below the bone, and stopped at the fletching. It protruded from his coat sleeve as his body turned sideways and his gun flew out of his hand, landing in the high grass along the road. With his right hand, Shelby immediately reached around and grabbed the arrow by the nock end and slid it out of his arm, gritting his teeth and cursing at the pain and the shooter.

Jack saw that Shelby had been skewered once again. "Get in the truck, Shelby! I don't wanna be next!"

Joe was nocking a third arrow onto his string as Shelby grabbed Stan by the shirt collar. He forcefully dragged the young boy to the passenger's side of the truck, all the while shouting in anger and fear.

Stan screamed as Shelby threw him onto the floorboard of the truck.

"Dad! Help me! No!"

L.D.'s heart broke as he watched his boy vanish into the pickup in the clutches of the two wild men.

Jack's pistol glistened in the evening sun when he held it outside the driver's window in his left hand. Then he drove forward a few feet, next to L.D. and Bob, fully intending to finish the job Shelby was unable to complete.

As he came to full draw again, Joe guessed the distance to the cab of the truck to be very close to 40 yards. He placed his sight pin on Jack's left shoulder. The dread of doing what he had to do was erased by his hatred of the evil that was about to be done to his friends. He also quickly thought of Stan, who was unseen, laying on the floor of the cab under Shelby's feet. Praying that his young friend would be unharmed, Joe let the arrow fly, and the 30-inch aluminum bullet whizzed by Jack's left ear. It barely missed his shoulder and with a loud metallic bang hit the windowframe above the steering wheel, then richocheted straight downward and slammed into the floorboard. The shaft had broken in half, adding to the deafening noise. Jack was so surprised by the noise that he hit the accelerator. Dirt and gravel flew as the truck sped off and went out of sight around the bend, beyond Joe's pickup.

Like the silence that returns after a thundering tornado passes through, the scene was quiet once again. The dust hung silently in the air above the road as Bob and L.D. slowly stood to their feet and stared helplessly in the direction they had last seen Stan. At that moment, Joe ran to meet his friends. When they turned to see who was coming their faces were ashen. L.D.'s countenance made it painfully clear that he was in complete shock. "Joe, they've got my boy! Oh, God, please have mercy...they've got my boy!"

Bob and Joe looked at each other in silent agreement that they'd never heard more heart-wrenching words come from a man. Tears filled L.D.'s eyes as Joe put his arm around his friend's shoulder.

"What are we gonna do, fellows?" L.D. asked pitifully.

Joe quickly dug into his knee pocket, retrieved his phone, and pushed the power button. "We'll get your boy back, L.D.!" Joe said, offering his desperate friend a small ray of hope. "We've just got to get some help!"

Joe knew his attempt to make a call earlier that morning about 60 yards off the road, and against the hillside, had been unfruitful. Hoping the change in position would yield a stronger signal, he dialed 911. As he held the phone to his ear and waited, he said, "Bob, we know those guys are driving toward a 'T' in the road. If they go right, they'll go by your house. If they go left, they'll end up below us."

Bob nodded his head in agreement. "And going left puts them at Highway 12, just above the Currey River Bridge. Who knows which way they'll go after that?"

"Aha!" Joe announced. "Hallelujah! It's ringing!" As he waited anxiously for an answer, he looked at L.D., and his heart groaned in sorrow for the man who still stared in the direction of his captured son.

The scratchy, broken signal became clear as a welcomed female voice said, "911 operator. How may I assist you?"

"Hello! Yes, I have an emergency!"

"Yes, sir. Go ahead, please."

"There's been a shooting and a young boy has been kidnapped. A very serious situation has developed out here in the western side of Giles County about 18 or 20 miles from Grandville."

"Has anyone been injured? Do you need an ambulance?"

"No, ma'am, not seriously. We just really need the police!" Joe was grateful that someone was listening. "I believe we've encountered the two men who robbed Harper's Grocery last night. They disabled my truck and shot at me this morning. Now they've taken a Chevy pickup that belongs to my friend L.D. Hill. And they have his 12-year-old son, Stan, with them as a hostage!"

"Where are you exactly at this moment, sir?"

"The best way to tell you is that on the east end of the Currey River Bridge, there's a gravel road that goes north. Right now, L.D. Hill, Bob Gleason, and I are standing on it at a point halfway between Highway 12 and Mill Creek Road. It's called Six Mile Road."

"Sir, did you say Bob Gleason is with you?"

"Yes, ma'am!"

"I believe Trooper Wilson is at Mr. Gleason's residence right now. He went there to ask about the whereabouts of Joe Tanner. Would that happen to be you?"

Thankful that someone would ask about him, and that Lance was in the area, Joe answered the operator with a grateful sigh, "Yes, that's me!"

"Your family has called about you. I'll let them know you are okay. Now, Mr. Tanner, I need to get one more detail from you very quickly, and then I'll send you some assistance right away. What directions do I give to Trooper Wilson so he can get to you?"

"Tell Wilson to turn left out of Bob's driveway and head west. Have him take the next road that goes to the left. That's where he'll find us. Tell him that he just might see L.D. Hill's red Chevy pickup. The windows are shot out of it, and there's a kid in there with the two suspects. The driver is armed and, believe me, they're both dangerous. One of them has been wounded twice by hunting arrows."

The operator thanked Joe for the information and asked him to stay on the line.

"Ma'am, I need to hang up for a minute. One of us will call you back shortly," Joe said firmly.

"Please do so, Mr. Tanner. We don't want to lose contact with you."

Joe pushed the "end" button on the phone and handed it to Bob. "If you don't mind, try this thing in my truck. In the glove compartment you'll find the charger for it. It'll work even without the engine running. Plug it in, and get back on the line with the 911 operator. Stay low, just in case those guys come back through here. If they don't see anyone in the cab, they'll most likely go on by. Thanks to those guys, my truck isn't driveable so we have no transportation."

Joe continued forming a plan. "L.D., see if you can find that pistol that flew into the grass, then hide yourself and wait along the road here. If they do happen to come back through, you'll have a way to defend yourself. I'm going to go down through these woods to the road below us. If they didn't turn left at the 'T' in the road and haven't already circled around and headed back to Highway 12, they'll end up in an encounter with Trooper Wilson who's at Bob's house right now trying to find out where I am. Once they meet him, they'll probably turn around, which means they'll end up on the road where I'll be. Let's just hope they turned right when they got to Mill Creek Road! Pray for God's help, fellows. We need Him badly right now."

L.D. sighed deeply and looked down the road. "Especially Stan." Then he turned toward the edge of the gravel road and began to search for the gun. Bob quickly walked toward Joe's truck with the phone in his hand, and Joe headed downhill toward the road below them. As he pushed aside the limbs full of early October foliage, he whispered to himself, "God, make my heart strong and my mind sharp."

At the moment the three friends split up, L.D.'s old truck was bouncing along toward Bob's house on Mill Creek Road.

17

▸─‹•›─○─‹•›─◂

"Mrs. Tanner?" the voice on the phone asked.

"Yes, this is Evelyn Tanner."

"This is Trooper Barton from the Grandville Police Department."

Evelyn held her breath for a moment in expectation and fear. Then she asked, "What's the news?"

"A 911 operator received a call from your husband a few minutes ago. He is on Six Mile Road near Bob Gleason's farm. He also indicated that L.D. Hill and Bob Gleason are with him. They encountered the two men who robbed Harper's Grocery Store last evening. At this time, all we know is that the three of them are involved in a situation, along with a fourth person who was taken by the suspects. We're doing what we can to bring this situation to a close."

Evelyn struggled to maintain her composure. "Is anyone hurt?"

"We don't know for sure yet."

Evelyn continued. "Do you know who the kidnap victim is?"

"We can't release that information right now."

"Thank you for calling, officer." As Evelyn hung up the phone she whispered a prayer for her husband and the police involved. Then she remembered that L.D.'s son had gone fishing with his dad. *Stan must be the one kidnapped!* As she added Stan to her prayers, she punched in the Hills' home number.

"Central to car 5, do you copy?"

"This is car 5, come back," Wilson responded.

"We just got a call from Joe Tanner. He encountered the two suspects from the Harper Grocery Store robbery. If you are at or near the Bob Gleason farm, Mr. Tanner said they are possibly headed in that direction in a red Chevy truck. The vehicle has the front and rear windows shot out."

"10-4, central. I'm within eyesight of that residence right now."

"Be advised that the two men have a hostage in the truck. It is the 12-year-old son of L.D. Hill. His name is Stan, The driver is armed."

"10-4. Any more information?"

"Mr. Tanner said that his position is on Six Mile Road halfway between Highway 12 and Mill Creek Road, which is west of the Gleason farm. Take the first gravel road on the left."

"Anybody injured?" Wilson asked as he slowed to a stop in front of the Gleason home.

"Only one of the suspects is injured. Apparently Tanner shot him with his bow and arrows. The wounds are not life-threatening."

Wilson looked left out his window at the Gleason home, and all seemed to be well. "Central, I am going to roll on by the Gleason residence and continue toward Mr. Tanner's 10-20."

Carla responded, "Mrs. Tanner has been contacted regarding this situation. We are sending more units to the area as fast as possible. I'll call Mrs. Hill."

"10-4, central. I'm rolling!"

Bob retrieved the cigarette lighter power adapter from the glove compartment of Joe's truck, plugged one end into the base of the phone, then the other into the lighter socket. He stared at the unfamiliar contraption and was confused by all the buttons. The world of modern communication devices had eluded him, and he was puzzled about what to do. "Lord, I lack wisdom here!" he whispered as he searched the face of the phone.

He saw the power button and pressed it. The phone came to life. He pushed 911 and held it to his ear and waited. Nothing happened. He repeated the same steps. Still nothing in the earpiece. "I'm doin' somethin' wrong here," he nervously mumbled as he looked at the wide array of options. Finally he saw the word "send" on the green button and wondered if it was the right choice. He pushed it and once again put the phone to his ear. He felt technically accomplished and thankful when it rang and a voice on the other end said, "911 operator, how may I assist you?"

"Hello, this is Bob Gleason."

"Yes, Mr. Gleason," the operator answered. "Thank you for calling. What is your status?"

"I am inside Joe Tanner's truck on Six Mile Road. He suggested I call you and stay on the phone here with you."

"Yes, sir. I will connect you with an assistant. Please stay on the line until an officer arrives at your location."

"Will do, ma'am. Thanks for your help!"

L.D. had easily recovered the .357 and checked the cylinder to see if it was loaded. Three bullets remained, and he angrily whispered to himself, "I'll do whatever I have to...whatever it takes...to get Stan back."

Along with an intense anger, he felt despair welling up inside him as he realized that if his truck came by him, flying bullets would be the last thing Stan needed. As he stood by the road, he looked up to the sky, closed his eyes, and silently prayed, *What we need here is a miracle. God, please protect my boy...please! Give him a supernatural strength and fill his young mind with peace and wisdom. Guide him, Lord. Please bring him back safely to us!*

When he came to the edge of the road below Six Mile, Joe found a huge clump of leafy brush that he used to conceal himself. It gave him a vantage point from which he could clearly see about 500 yards in either direction. As he panted from the nearly half-mile downhill run, he nocked his last arrow onto the string, took a practice draw, and anxiously watched and intently listened as the late-afternoon sun headed toward the horizon. In the stillness of the countryside he thought of Evelyn and his kids, whom he hoped had received the news of his whereabouts. He knew they would be relieved for only a moment, only until they learned of his encounter with "Donnie and Clyde."

His emotions were suddenly swept up in a vicious wave of dread as he thought of young Stan Hill stuck in the cab of his dad's old truck with the two dangerous strangers. He wondered where they were, and he offered a quiet prayer: "God, give us peace in the face of this enemy. It'll be a sign of defeat to those guys if You'll give us peace. We're not wrestling with flesh and blood here, Lord. This battle is in another realm. Only You can help us!"

As Joe whispered "amen" at the end of his heartfelt cry, he thought of a comparison between his situation and another familiar story. He soberly said to himself, "If they come down this road I'll have only one stone to throw at this Goliath. It better be a good shot!"

Earl Potter left his home on Bender's Gap Road and turned right on Mill Creek. He had no idea he was only one minute behind Trooper Wilson. Earl had decided to go to Bob's house and seek his seasoned wisdom. As he thought of the risky trips he had already made to the Currey River Bridge, he comforted himself by saying, "Surely the old gentleman will help me. He'll listen to me. He'll believe my story. I know I can trust him!"

As Earl came over a rise in the road and the Gleason farm came into view, he caught a glimpse of a patrol car making the turn in the bend that was beyond Bob's house about a quarter of a mile. His heart fluttered in fearful excitement when he faced the likelihood that the search for Jack and Shelby had moved into the area. Earl stopped his Chevy 4x4 in the gravel road to think for a moment. Knowing that he faced an incredibly important choice, he softly worded a question he never thought he would.

"What would Sarah suggest I do in this moment?"

His heart knew the answer to the question, but he found it very difficult to let it find a resting place in his mind. Admitting to himself that the time had come in his life to find a lasting peace, he whispered, "She'd tell me to face the music…and speak the truth. All I can do is hope for mercy. I'm tired of running!" With that major milestone reached in his heart, Earl decided to chase down the patrol car and offer his assistance in the pursuit of the two outlaws. As Earl pressed the accelerator under his foot, he suddenly felt a level of calmness he had not felt in many years.

At that very moment, Jack and Shelby were heading toward an unexpected rendezvous with Trooper Wilson.

18

When Jack arrived at the intersection of Six Mile and Mill Creek Roads, he barked at Stan, "Sit up, kid!"

Stan sat up and looked over the dash at his surroundings. As Jack held the steering wheel in his left hand, with his right he grabbed Stan by the shirt collar and pulled him toward his face. He demanded, "You need to tell us which way to go here, you little twit. And you'd better tell the truth! You know this area, don't you?"

"Yes, sir." Stan answered with a trembling voice, nearly gagging at the smell of Jack's breath. "If you go right, it'll take you to Highway 12 in about four or five miles." He thought about telling them that a left turn would be a quicker way to the main road, but he took comfort in leading the two men on a route where at least he knew there were houses. Jack let go of Stan, and Shelby forcefully pushed him back to the floor of the truck. "Stay down, you little twerp. And don't even think about gettin' up!"

When Jack turned right onto Mill Creek Road and accelerated, the truck swerved left and right in the gravel. Jack angrily yelled at Shelby as the wind whipped through the open windshield. "The kid's our ticket out of here, Shelby. Try not to hurt him! Here…make yourself useful, and reload my gun."

As Shelby opened the cylinder of the .357 and loaded three more rounds, his voice turned to a wolflike growl. "This stupid kid must be the son of that L.D. guy. I'm gonna take great pleasure in usin' this little squirt to make his daddy's buddy, *Mr. Robin Hood*, regret he ever saw my face!" As Shelby said the words, he handed the pistol back to Jack, pulled his coat off for the first time since his second injury, and reluctantly looked at his wound.

Jack glanced for a moment at Shelby's bloody coat sleeve and shook his head in halfhearted sympathy. "How's your arm?"

"Arms, man! *Arms!* Both of 'em are hurtin' really bad. Feels like somebody poked a hot brandin' iron down in my left one. I've gotta get somethin' to clean these holes!"

Jack ignored Shelby's self-prognosis and went on to a matter he felt was more serious.

"I hope those guys don't find that gun you lost back there. It's got your fingerprints all over it!"

Without saying a word, Shelby looked straight ahead. The sudden rush of fear at the thought of leaving behind such incriminating evidence was more painful than the stinging in his arms.

Jack gripped the steering wheel extra tight and wiped his eyes from the dust that was coming through the broken window in front of him. "We're in this thing deeper than I intended, but we can't turn back. We may have to go out in a blaze of glory, ole buddy, but I ain't goin' back to the pen!"

As Stan lay on the floor, wondering what would happen to him, he was shaking with fear. His right cheek was pressed to the rubber mat, and as he faced the underside of the bench on the passenger side he felt Shelby's heavy foot on his back.

As Shelby's tennis shoe pressed onto his spine, holding him firmly to the floor, Stan suddenly felt a calmness that surprised him, and he boldly spoke up. "Mister, would you kindly take your foot off my back? It sure is making things rougher down here."

"I said shut up, kid! One more word and I'll hang you out the window by your feet and drag your little ugly face on the road!"

As Stan's jaw bounced on the rubber mat, his eyes fell on an item under the bench that brought hope to his heart. One of his dad's knives was tucked away in a black leather sheath with a Velcro latch. It had a four-inch folding blade and was compact enough for Stan's pants pocket. He slowly moved his arm toward it. Without being noticed because of the jostling ride, he wrapped his fingers around the case. To avoid the swooshing sound of separating Velcro, he slowly opened the cover. He quietly took the knife out of its sheath and, without being detected, slid it into the left pocket of his pants. He continued to stare under the seat.

Another item caught his eye. It was an old green nylon fish stringer about six feet in length. It had a rusted metal guide on one end and a quarter-sized metal loop on the other. As he slowly moved his arm toward the stringer, he saw before him a grand opportunity in the form of a large loop in one of the lacings in Shelby's tennis shoes. *If I could somehow connect this stringer from his shoelace to this seat, it might help me escape if I get a chance to run. But I need both hands to do it.*

Hoping the man who was driving would come to his defense again, Stan spoke up once more. "Mister, would you mind if I turned over on my side?"

Shelby clenched his fist and held it in front of Stan's face. Jack could tell that the boy was about to get a beating.

"Let him do it, Shelby. He can't hurt anything, and he'll stop talkin'."

Shelby glared at Jack then reluctantly eased the pressure. With the freedom to move, Stan wiggled his way onto his side in a fetal position, which allowed him to reach with both arms under the truck bench.

This is great! he thought, as he began to anchor his assailant to his dad's truck. *I've got to leave him enough slack to be able to shuffle his feet without knowing he's connected.* Feeling surprised again, yet confident with the idea, he gradually slid the metal guide that was designed for a fish's mouth, up and over the curled spring supporting the underside of the bench, then slipped it through the metal ring. As the two men above him loudly talked back and forth, he pulled the six remaining feet of string on through, leaving enough length to attach to Shelby's shoelace. With the same care a doctor would give to closing an incision after surgery, he carefully slipped the guide through the lacing of Shelby's shoe that was next to the door. As the truck bounced on the bumpy country road, Stan fought to steady his hands. Within two minutes, he succeeded in tying the nylon string into a knot. Shelby was oblivious to the trap! Stan whispered assuring words to himself: *I'll get away from these guys. I know I will. God, please help me!*

Bill Foster gassed up his new hunter-green Suburban and headed west on Highway 12. About five miles out of town he dialed his home number.

"Donna, I had to run by the office and get my charged battery for my cell. Plus I had to get some gas before leaving town. Now, I'm on my way to Bob's. Have you heard anything since I left the house?"

"Yes. Thank goodness you called. I just heard from Evelyn a few minutes ago. Joe's been located! He got tangled up with those two crooks on the run, but he's okay. The two thieves grabbed a hostage though. Evelyn thinks it might be Stan Hill."

"You're kidding, Donna!" Bill's silence that followed his response revealed his shock. Bracing himself for the answer, he asked, "Where are Joe and L.D.?"

"I'm not quite sure, except I know they're still out in the Gleason farm area."

Donna had no intention of trying to stop Bill from assisting his friends. Knowing that Joe and L.D. would do the same for her husband, she added, "Honey, I know you want to help out there. Do you think you should…It's dangerous…should you take something…"

"To protect myself with?" Bill guessed, a little surprised that Donna was suggesting he have some firepower.

"Yes, sweetheart. I just hope you don't get hurt out there."

"If I had known about the mess everyone is in I might have brought along my .38, but I didn't. I don't want to delay getting out to the Gleason farm, so I'll just keep going."

Donna started to speak, but Bill announced, "While I was pumping gas I did notice my birthday gift is still in the back of the 'Burban."

"You have your crossbow?"

"Yep," Bill answered confidently.

"Are you good with it, yet?"

"Well, I haven't hunted with it, but I've shot it enough to feel confident. There are four bolts in the quiver. I don't think I'll have to use it, but if I have to, I can."

Donna didn't find a lot of consolation in Bill's limited experience with his new "toy" and thought of a more comforting idea. "Bill, I think the best weapon we have at this point is prayer. We can use our 'Cross-bow'!"

Donna's attempt to ease the tension with a little bit of divine humor went over the head of her preoccupied husband, who simply answered, "I love ya, babe. I'll see you after a while." Donna hung up the phone and sat down on a stool in her den. She stared out her bay window, then offered a quiet prayer for Bill and their friends.

Matthew Tanner paced the floor for several minutes and finally spoke in a tone that startled Evelyn and his sisters, who were sitting at the kitchen table.

"We've gotta do something, Mom! We can't just sit here. It'll be dark in a couple of hours, and Dad's still out there. Stan's in danger and here we sit! Can't we do anything besides sit here like *zombies*?"

With her elbows on their round, oak kitchen table, Evelyn bowed her head and placed her fingertips on her temples. The volume of her son's voice, which was normally subdued, revealed the strain and fear that gripped him. She looked up at Matthew and stared briefly into his young eyes. "I'm with you, Matt. I want to do something, too—anything but sit here!"

"Well, why don't we go? We're worthless here. We know that area around Mr. Gleason's farm. Maybe we could help the police navigate it!"

Evelyn was suspended in the vast space between sitting like a slug at home and going off to help her beloved. She suddenly decided it was time to move into action. She stood up and spoke words that surprised herself, as well as her children.

"Okay, girls, you stay here and tend to the phone. Matt and I are going for a drive. I know the roads, and he knows the woods since he's been there many times." Evelyn ran her hands through her shoulder-length brown hair and briefly looked at the ceiling as she planned her next move.

"I'm going next door to see if the Carsons will loan me their cell phone. Matt, you open the garage door and start the van." At that command, Evelyn disappeared out the front door of the house.

Matthew stood motionless for a moment in total and joyful shock at hearing his mother sound so sergeantlike. He then wheeled around on his heels and walked quickly to the key rack mounted next to the refrigerator. He felt a closeness to his mother in that moment that is only generated by crisis.

Within five minutes, Evelyn returned with the Carsons' fully charged phone in her hand. "Bessie, you're in charge here. Keep the phone line open. Don't have long conversations with anyone. We'll be at this number." She handed her oldest daughter a piece of paper with the Carsons' cell number on it. "We'll be back soon!" Both girls stood side by side as Evelyn walked out the door. They looked at each other as if to ask, "Was that our mother?"

Evelyn instructed her son to get behind the wheel of the minivan. "I want you to drive, Matt, in case I need to make some calls. I know this situation has you all keyed up, but you've got to stay calm and concentrate on the road. I know in my heart that your dad needs our help. I don't want us to get in the way of the law, but if we can help your dad, L.D., Stan, and Bob, we'll do what we can. Are you ready to go?"

Matthew's eyes showed a confidence that was beyond his years as he answered his mother. "Yes! Let's do it!"

Evelyn reached up to push the "close" button on her garage remote mounted above the visor. As she felt for the button, her fingers touched the cold, round, metal cylinder of mace that was clipped behind the remote.

"Well, well, Matt. Look what I have." Evelyn held up the slender, four-inch-tall can and smiled as Matthew looked her way.

"Ah!" Matthew mused as he looked back at the road ahead of him. "Dog spray for your walks with Dad. Have you had to use it on that snot-nosed beast that moved in down the street?"

"Not yet. But I have a feeling I will sooner or later!"

Evelyn attached the can to her leather belt. As she did, she patted it with her right hand, cocked her jaw, made a sniffing sound, and spoke with a Barney Fife-type sigh. "I think I'll just clip this baby on my belt...just in case."

Matthew chuckled at her "Barney" impersonation. He knew who Barney was from reruns. As he pressed down on the turn signal, he asked, "Mom?"

"Yes, son."

"Don't you think you ought to go ahead and put your bullet in it?"

Both of them nervously laughed as they drove toward the Gleason farm.

19

▸━◈━○━◈━◂

Jack suddenly hit the brakes. "We've got problems, Shelby! We're gonna have to turn around and make a run for it!" he yelled as he pointed at the patrol car ahead of them.

Shelby challenged the idea. "Hey, let's try going on by that cop. He don't know who we are. Just be calm and slide on by him!"

Jack's voice sounded skeptical. "Maybe it's worth a try. Just keep the kid quiet, and out of sight."

Thirty seconds later the patrol car and L.D.'s pickup were nearly nose to nose. Wilson's heart pounded in his chest with fearful excitement as he realized he was face-to-face with the two fugitives the city of Grandville desperately wanted behind bars. Though he could see only a pair of heads in the cab, he knew he had to assume the boy was still in the truck. In a friendly manner, he slowed, put his arm out the window, and waved for the pickup to go on by.

"Jack, I believe he thinks we're locals," Shelby loudly whispered with his face straight ahead but eyes turned to see the police. "Go on by and wave thank you, and let's get out of here. We can fool this guy! Just keep your gun handy in case somethin' goes wrong."

Jack started to slip by the patrol car. He slowed to avoid appearing too anxious to pass, and when the vehicles were hood to hood, Wilson leaned his head out to speak to the strangers. Jack didn't want to do it,

185

but he decided it would be best to oblige the officer. He brought the pickup to a stop. The two vehicles sat side by side, window to window.

Wilson called on all of his training as a lawman and calmly addressed the men in the truck. "Howdy, fellows. What's happenin' today?"

"Not much, officer. What brings you to these parts?"

As he looked from bumper to bumper of the truck, Wilson responded, "Just came out to give Mr. Gleason a visit. Say, what happened to your truck?" Wilson quickly added a cover for the question he had just asked to see how the driver would respond. "Did that storm that hit us two nights ago do that damage?" Giles County hadn't had a serious storm in over two weeks.

"Yes, sir!" Jack was relieved that the cop had given him a way to explain the missing windshields. "That was one whale of a storm. Took a tree out—and our windows with it!"

Wilson was amazed at how calm and collected the suspect seemed. He looked around Jack and saw that the passenger wasn't showing quite the same amount of composure. In an effort to further convince the two that he was not aware of their identity, and to protect the young boy, he asked, "Are you the Johnson brothers who live off of Highway 12? You sure do favor Richard." Wilson pulled a name out of his memory from a time when he'd lived on the other side of the state.

Jack was weary of the questions that were holding him back. Still, he felt it necessary to accommodate the officer. "Yeah, he's our uncle."

Wilson noticed the passenger seemed to press something down with his arms and held it there. He imagined he had a hand over the boy's mouth and decided it would be best to end the conversation, calmly drive away, then call central on his radio. "Well, I guess you'll be gettin' those windows fixed. Otherwise, you'll be eatin' a lot of bugs!"

As Wilson was speaking, he looked in his rearview mirror and saw a white Chevy approaching. It triggered the memory of Carla's call about the vehicle spotted at the nearby bridge the previous evening. *I wonder who that is?* Before he pressed his accelerator, Lance offered one more statement to the pair he wished he could handcuff, "Hey, you all be careful. There's two men on the run from the law somewhere in the area. They're armed and dangerous. You haven't seen anybody like that, have you?"

"Oh…no, sir. But if we do, we'll give you a call right away." Jack smiled with an expression that made Wilson's skin crawl.

Jack and Shelby were so rattled and preoccupied with getting by the cop that neither of them noticed the white vehicle that was approaching until it was nearly by them. Jack looked sharply to his right to hide his face.

Earl was so nervous about connecting with the officer that the sight of the damaged pickup didn't register in his mind. As a result, the two acquaintances managed to pass without recognizing each another.

When the truck was less than 20 yards behind him, Wilson reached for his radio mic and pressed the button. "Car 5 to central. Carla, do you copy?"

"10-4, car 5. Go ahead."

"Do you have help on the way? I just spent a few minutes with the suspects. I believe they still have the boy, so I didn't attempt an arrest. It would've been too dangerous."

"There is a unit moving your way at this moment. It should be really close to you right now."

Wilson reported, "I've got a white Chevy 4x4 behind me here on Mill Creek Road. That rings a bell!"

Suddenly, another transmission broke into the conversation with Carla. "Wilson, do you copy?"

"This is Wilson. Go ahead!"

"This is Jackson. We're five minutes from the Gleason place, rollin' at a good pace. What's your 20?"

"I'm west of the Gleason farm. I just encountered the suspects, and they're headed your way. Don't turn your lights on. I'm certain they've got the boy."

"10-4, Wilson. We're alerted to the situation!" Jackson turned off his flashing lights.

Jack was rolling at about 50 miles per hour as he drove by the Gleason residence and disappeared over the rise in the road. Shelby held his left arm and his moans caused by the throbbing pain went unheard above the noisy ride.

When Wilson looked in his rearview mirror and saw that the red pickup was out of his sight behind him, he made a quick U-turn in a grassy area. When he drove by the Chevy, he looked at the driver. It wasn't someone he knew.

Well beyond the Gleason driveway, Jack suddenly hit the brakes and started sliding side to side. Shelby looked up and saw a second patrol car coming toward them. "They're here, man. They know we're in the area. That cop back there knew who we were all along! Turn around, Jack!"

Jack shoved the gearshift into reverse and moved backward, breaking some small trees that edged the road. Then he dropped the shift into drive and spun out as he sped back toward Wilson's car. As soon as he regained control of the pickup, he saw Wilson's unit coming his way.

"I've got them in sight, Jackson!" Wilson radioed, as he felt for his weapon.

When Jack met Wilson's patrol car again on the road, he made no attempt to slow down. He rolled the truck up onto the short bank on the right side of the road, tore through the barbed wire fence, and drove into the field at the road's edge. When Jack went around Wilson's car, he saw the white 4x4 that followed. As the two passed one another, Jack got a glimpse of the familiar face behind the wheel. He grunted with disgust and briefly wished he could go after the ex-in-law who had stood him up at the Currey River Bridge the night before. Instead, once he was beyond the two vehicles, Jack gave the steering wheel a left jerk, bounced back onto Mill Creek Road, slammed the accelerator down, and sped off. By then Earl realized who was in the beat-up truck the officer was so intent on stopping. Without thinking twice about it, he decided to join the pursuit.

Unaware of the chase that had developed three-and-a-half miles away, Joe stood motionless in the quiet of the roadside. The lower limb of his compound rested in the waist-belt holster. As he held it upright with his right hand, he reached into his left pocket to retrieve his watch to check the time. When he pulled the watch out, along with it came a portion of his pink tracking ribbon. He started to stuff it back into his pocket, but hesitated. He looked at the ribbon, and suddenly he got an idea.

20

❧

Jack was nearing the intersection of Six Mile Road when Shelby looked over at him and waved his arm to signal him to keep going straight. They flew on by the familiar road.

"Don't kill us, Jack! I don't wanna die in the country!"

Jack had gone another half mile when he came to a 90-degree bend in the road. He slowed barely enough to negotiate the turn. As he slid sideways, he accelerated and headed south on the road that led to the Currey River Bridge, where they'd ended up the night before in old man Scutter's truck. He was less than two minutes from Joe's position. Troopers Wilson and Jackson were not far behind and closing fast.

L.D. knelt on the roadside and clutched the half-loaded .357 he'd found. In the silence, he imagined the hand that had once held the weapon. Hatred stirred in his heart. His thoughts turned to Tricia and his head spun with sickening emotion. He assumed she had heard about Stan's dangerous predicament. He whispered to himself, "Let one of us be a weapon in your hands, God! Help us get my boy back!"

Bob was sitting in Joe's truck with the cell phone to his ear. Suddenly a voice broke the silence. "Mr. Gleason, do you have a report for me? What do you see or hear?"

He sat up and looked around. "Just silence here. The birds are singing because they don't know what's goin' on. Makes me envious."

"Yes, sir, I can certainly understand that." The operator added, "Please stay on the line. I'll get back to you in a few minutes."

Joe ran from the middle of the road and back to the position he had been holding earlier. He picked up his bow, renocked his last arrow, and listened intently. Suddenly a sound faded up in the distance. It was the familiar noise of gravel crunching under the weight of a heavy vehicle. It was accompanied by the low roar of an engine. His pulse doubled as he raised his bow and pointed it in the direction of the commotion.

Bill knew he was speeding as he tightly held the wheel of his Suburban. He reached across the seat, grabbed his phone, and dialed Joe's number. Hearing the busy signal, Bill decided to call 911 and report his whereabouts.

"911 operator, how may I assist you?"

"Yes, ma'am. This is Bill Foster. I'm a friend of Joe Tanner, L.D. Hill, and Bob Gleason. Right now I'm in the area near Gleason's farm in western Giles County."

"Mr. Foster, I have Bob Gleason on the line with me. Would you like to relay a message to him?"

"Please tell Bob I am on my way. I should be in the area in about 15 or 20 minutes. Can you tell me where he is?"

The operator asked Bill to hold, and a few moments later she returned. "Mr. Foster, Bob said that he and L.D. Hill are on Six Mile Road halfway between Mill Creek and Highway 12."

"Tell him I'll join him there as quickly as I can. And by the way, I'm driving a green Suburban." Bill quickly pressed his "end" button to avoid the possibility of receiving instructions from the operator to stay away from the area. He was intent on helping his friends.

Bob called out to L.D. through the open window of Joe's truck. "Hey, L.D., come up here!"

L.D. looked up and down the road and saw that it was clear. He walked to Joe's truck, and Bob announced the good news that they would soon be joined by a familiar face.

At that moment, Wilson sped by the Six Mile Road intersection and headed toward the sharp turn Jack had barely negotiated.

Evelyn looked anxiously out the front window of the minivan as she and her son passed the sign that marked the west edge of town. "Matt, I know you never dreamed you'd hear me say this, but could you drive a little faster? You're not 'Driving Miss Daisy' today!"

"Wow, Mom, those really are strange words...coming from you," Matt responded, as he pressed the accelerator.

As they drove toward Mill Creek Road, Evelyn relieved the tension by offering her son a conversational distraction.

"Matt, do you like the food we've been eating lately?"

"I sure do. I like it a lot. But there is one thing I'll have to admit. I miss having a good dose of grease every once in a while. Since you started cooking for Dad's heart, I suspect we're all gonna live to be 200 years old. Don't get me wrong, I know it's best for us, but sometimes my stomach wants junk food!"

"I miss the fat grams, too," Evelyn agreed.

"Mom, if I have a 'grease craving', I know where to feed it."

Evelyn looked at Matt in shock. "And where would that be?"

"Jim's market. They sell corn dogs, and there's enough fat in one of those belly-bombs to last me about a month!"

"Do you actually do that?" Evelyn's voice revealed her surprise.

"I've been known to do it on occasion," Matt admitted, then looked at his mother to see if her expression revealed any evidence of having been offended. "Are you upset?"

"No. Are you?"

As Matthew laughed at his mama's quick wit, Evelyn conceded with a motherly sigh, "I suppose I should be happy that at least it's not drugs you're going for." It was a satisfying feeling to know that she and her young son were still able to communicate. Then she thought of how much she hoped Tricia would be able to talk again with Stan.

Lance Wilson's mind swarmed with strategies as he drove toward the sharp turn 50 yards ahead. When he finally saw the 90-degree turn, it was too late. He dropped the radio mic and grabbed the wheel with both hands. His front tires bounced through the ditch and went airborne. The car landed on the three-foot embankment, causing the rear end to bounce wildly upward before landing hard. Wilson fought to make the left turn. His speed quickly sent him sideways into the field, and the right front and rear tires dug into the soft soil. Suddenly the left side of the vehicle raised off the ground. As black dirt and soybean plants flew by his right window, Wilson put his hands on the roof. Within seconds, he was hanging upside down, held in place by his seat belt. He quickly assessed his health and decided he was unharmed except for his left thumb, which he'd jammed against the roof.

He had the presence of mind to turn off the car engine. When he did, he heard another engine running nearby. After wrestling with the seat belt, it unlatched and Wilson fell to the roof of the car. He shot a quick glance at the feet running toward his wrecked unit. He looked past the feet and saw the familiar white Chevy parked at the edge of the road. He quickly grabbed his pistol, crawled halfway out of the overturned car, and looked up. "Stop right there!" he yelled.

Earl stopped in his tracks. "It's okay, officer, I'm on your side. I know what's going on, and I just want to help!"

As Wilson crawled out onto the ground, he looked beyond the Chevy and saw Trooper Jackson's car pulling up. Then he looked back at Earl. "Who are you, mister?"

"My name is Earl Potter. I'm a relative...actually an ex-relative... to one of those guys you're chasing. It's a long story, but believe me, I want to get those guys as much as you do!"

Jackson ran up to the two men standing by Wilson's wrecked unit and looked at his disheveled fellow trooper. "Are you okay, Lance?"

"I'll be fine. Those two guys are just in front of us. We've gotta go!"

Wilson and Jackson started to run to the remaining patrol car to continue their pursuit of the suspects, when Earl interrupted.

"Officers, I know you're in a hurry but let me quickly tell you that

I live around here, and one of those guys is my former brother-in-law from Chicago. He called me last night and wanted me to help them get out of the county. I hate to admit it, but I started to help them out. Something went wrong, and to be honest, I'm glad it did. I never did connect with them. I'll explain it to you later. Is there anything I can do right now to help you get them into custody?"

Jackson looked at Wilson, who was rattled by the wreck. "What do you think, Wilson? Do we need this man's help?"

As he brushed the dirt off his pants, Wilson gave Earl some instructions. "We'd be grateful if you'd go back by Bob Gleason's farm and on to the end of Mill Creek. If you see any patrol cars on the way, wave them down and give them directions to our location."

Jackson looked at his partner and slightly grinned as he butted in. "And tell them about this 90-degree turn!"

Wilson dropped his head for a moment, graciously accepted the ribbing, and finished. "If you get to Highway 12 and haven't seen any other units, wait there a while, and then go on over to the Currey River Bridge and wait there. Do you have a phone?"

"No, sir. I'm sorry, I sure don't." Even without the ability to stay in contact with them, Earl enjoyed the good feeling of knowing he was actually being asked to assist.

Jack slowed the truck down and Shelby looked up with a puzzled expression on his face. "Why are we stopping, Jack? I think we've lost 'em, but this is not a good time to stop!"

Jack leaned forward and wiped his eyes with the back of his hand. "What is that?" He was referring to some pink ribbon that mysteriously hovered above the road about five feet high and parallel to the ground. He was too far away to see the thin string Joe had attached to each end and tied to a tree on one side of the road and a fence post on the other. Hanging from it, exactly in the middle of the road, was a five-inch square of white paper.

Shelby gazed at the sight. "That's weird, Jack! Is the road closed?"

"It can't be. I think we were just through here last night. I believe I know where we are now! Right back there looks like where we finally came out of those stupid fields by the river and got onto this gravel road. I'm tellin' you, we were here just last night, and it was open all the way to the pavement. This road will take us back to the bridge."

Jack turned his head to check the road behind them then slowly pulled the truck to within 30 feet of the pink obstruction. He leaned forward with his chest on the steering wheel. With a surprised look on his face, he turned to Shelby. "Hey, are my eyes deceiving me or does that paper have my name on it?"

Shelby quickly glanced at it. "It sure does. Maybe your buddy Tony put it there."

Jack opened his door and got out. As he approached the ribbon, he saw the thin twine that held it in place. He threw his hands up in embarrassed disbelief. As he reached for the paper, Joe came to full draw about 35 yards behind them.

Jack held the paper sideways and saw that his name had been scribbled on it in large letters with black ink over what appeared to be some type of official form. Under his name in smaller letters was written, "Please turn the paper over." When he looked on the other side, his blood chilled as he read the words out loud. "I have you in my sights." It was signed...*Robin Hood!*

21

Jack quickly let go of the note that Joe had written on the back of his hunting license. He hastily looked around in all directions, and then, in an effort to make himself a hard target for the concealed archer, he crouched down and started darting back and forth on his way back to the truck. Just the thought of being run through by an arrow was much too painful to deal with.

Shelby was bewildered at the sight of his friend acting like a bug around a light bulb. "What are you doin' out there, Jack?"

"You better get low, Shelby, if you don't want another hole poked in you," Jack yelled as he hurriedly came around the truck and nervously slid into the driver's seat. With his head just high enough to see above the dash, he quickly put the truck in gear, and started toward the ribbon. Shelby couldn't help but shiver at the thought of hearing the snap of the bow again.

Joe heard the click of the transmission, and before Jack could press the gas pedal the last of the archer's four arrows was in flight. His white pin was resting on the left rear tire when he released the string. The sharp field tip of the arrow found its mark. The shaft penetrated the rubber tire and was sticking out about 10 inches, acting like a plug. However, when Jack rolled the truck forward, the arrow broke in the gravel, and the sudden, familiar, loud whooshing sound of a deflating tire caused Jack to hesitate.

In the confusion of the moment, Jack hit the gas and the truck fishtailed left and right, then plunged into the ditch on the side of the road. The frame that hung lower than normal due to the flat tire lodged firmly in the ditch. Jack tried unsuccessfully to back out. Frustrated and angry because they were stuck and the nearby hunter was probably going to shoot another aluminum missile, Jack felt they had only one option.

"Shelby, we've gotta run for it. I'm not gonna get this thing out of this ditch. You grab the kid and let's hit the woods. Just keep moving if you don't wanna get poked again!"

Jack quickly opened his door and hit the ground running, thrashing into the cover of the brush that lined the road. He didn't bother to turn around as he tore through the thick woods and ran out of sight up the hill.

Shelby threw his door open and quickly attempted to exit the truck. When he did, the six feet of thin, green line stretched tight and caused him to fall facedown onto the gravel road. Seeing Shelby still attached to the seat in the cab by one leg and lying awkwardly on the ground, Stan saw his chance to escape. He stood on the seat and jumped high over Shelby's back and onto the ground beyond him. He took off running toward the rear of his dad's pickup. As he rounded the tailgate, he gasped when he saw another person running toward him. Stan was relieved and grateful when he recognized the partially painted face of Joe Tanner.

"He's tied to the truck, Mr. Tanner!" Stan excitedly announced. "He doesn't have a gun, but the other guy does!"

At that news, Joe quickly looked across the road to make sure Jack wasn't returning and then cautiously looked around the truck. He saw that Shelby was wrestling with a small rope that held him to the cab like a leash. Without hesitating, Joe came to full draw again, even though his quiver and bow were empty. He stepped to within five feet of the unarmed crook. With the sun behind him and knowing that Shelby would have to look up into the light, Joe guessed that his captive wouldn't be able to tell that the bow rest didn't have an arrow in it. He stared across his bowstring at the struggling suspect. "Stay right where you are, mister, or I'll pin you to the ground!"

Shelby looked up at Joe, who was standing ominously over him with the bow pointed right at his face. The fear of looking at the vicious-looking contraption and feeling another arrow in him motivated Shelby to abandon his attempt to escape. He put his head back on the gravel.

As Joe swung around to ensure that Shelby wouldn't be able to detect that his bow wasn't loaded, he heard another vehicle approaching the scene. "Whoever it is, Stan, wave them down!"

"Mr. Tanner, it's the police!"

Shelby groaned at the news, and Joe said a familiar word, as he looked beyond Stan at the dark-gray patrol car. "*Yes!*"

Jackson stopped his vehicle at the rear of the red pickup that was stuck by the road. Both troopers quickly exited and pulled their weapons out of their holsters.

"Lance, you're a sight for sore eyes!" Joe said while relaxing the tension on his bow. "Man, I didn't know if I could keep this thing at full draw for another minute." Joe looked down at Shelby, caught his eye, and mockingly announced, "Even though it *wasn't loaded!*" When Shelby saw there was no arrow on the string, he grabbed a handful of gravel and threw it at the truck in defeated disgust. He moaned as he clutched his aching left arm.

Wilson pointed his gun at Shelby. "Who you got there, Mr. Tanner?"

As he held the bow down at his side, Joe responded, "This is the yahoo who emptied his weapon at me this morning. It's a wonder I'm still alive. I can prove he's the one who shot at me. There's a hole in each of his arms. I personally put them there. The other guy took off up the hill through the woods!" Joe looked anxiously in the direction of his unsuspecting friends waiting on the road above him.

Jackson walked back to his patrol car, radioed to central, and reported the turn of events. Trooper Wilson replaced his pistol in his holster, knelt over Shelby, and proceeded to secure his prisoner's arms behind his back. As he did, he looked at the nylon string that was still tied to Shelby's shoe. "Whose idea was this?"

"That was mine," Stan said proudly. "Would you like for me to cut him free for you? I have a knife."

"If you don't mind, little buddy, I'd appreciate it," Wilson responded, and he continued his praise of Stan's clever trap that had snared Shelby. "Looks like you caught yourself a big fish today!"

"Yes, sir. I reckon so."

Shelby glared at Stan as the young man proudly walked over, pulled the knife out of his pocket, tugged it open, and ran the blade through the stringer.

Stan was watching with widened eyes as Jackson helped Shelby up then manhandled him toward the patrol car. Wilson grinned when he saw the boy's amazed expression. "I don't think we'll use the catch and release method on this fish. What do you think, little buddy?"

Stan answered the trooper with a smile. "No, sir, we won't!"

With Shelby confined securely in the caged backseat, Jackson communicated with Carla and hung his microphone back in its clip.

"Wilson, looks like there's another unit and a wrecker on the way. When they get here, we can send this guy on to jail and let them take the boy home to his family. Then we can join in the search for the other suspect. Also, there's another fellow on his way to this area by the name of Bill Foster. He's a friend of Joe Tanner's, and he's in a green Suburban." Jackson exited his patrol car and looked around for Joe. The camo-clad hunter was nowhere in sight.

"Where did Joe Tanner go?" Jackson inquired.

Wilson looked in all directions and immediately assumed that Joe had gone after the other suspect. Unaware that Joe felt intensely responsible for L.D. and Bob's safety, the two troopers had not noticed that he had stashed his bow in the bed of the pickup and quietly slipped off to help his friends. Joe was also driven by the memory of the distraught look on L.D.'s face when Stan had been forcefully snatched away by Jack and Shelby. He was determined that L.D. would not have to wait one minute longer than necessary to hear that his son was in safe hands.

"Well," Wilson said with an understanding sigh, "at least he's dressed for the dangerous journey. May the Lord protect him...especially when Evelyn hears about this!"

As Joe cautiously headed up the hillside through the early October woods he was being slapped in the face by low-hanging branches. He stopped to rest and to carefully listen for any audible signs of Jack's presence. Confident that the way was clear, he pressed on. He guessed that he was within seven to ten minutes of Bob and L.D., and he was hoping he'd come out on the road near his disabled truck. Little did Joe know that only a few minutes earlier, Jack had wandered up the hill across the very same path.

22

‣•❖•◂‣

Only 80 minutes of full daylight remained when Jack stumbled onto the edge of Six Mile Road. He was hyperventilating as he looked up and down the lane to see if it was clear. Not really caring whether or not Shelby managed to escape with their young hostage, Jack's focus turned to survival.

As he stood alone in the open space of the gravel road, he pulled out his .357 and made sure it was fully loaded. Then he mentally retraced the steps he and Shelby had taken that day and determined that he was back on the road where he had first encountered the bowhunter. He recalled that when he and Shelby had approached the blue-and-white truck they had disabled, they were walking uphill. Jack decided that if he walked to the right on the road and headed downhill, he would eventually return to the bridge and at least be reunited with the money stashed under it. He didn't know that only 400 yards around the bend, the two men he had left behind in a mad rush were standing by, waiting for Bill to arrive. As he walked south on Six Mile Road, he suddenly heard a vehicle approaching behind him.

The police! Jack thought as he quickly jumped into the brushy edge of the road and hid.

As the vehicle slowly rounded the turn, Jack saw that it was not a patrol car, but a large, dark-green Suburban. He heaved a sigh of relief and stood motionless as it slowly rolled by. Once the rig passed him, Jack ran to the rear window and slapped it twice with his hand. The brake lights came on, and Bill came to a stop.

Assuming it was one of his buddies, Bill lowered his window and looked over his left shoulder. Without warning, he was staring down the barrel of a huge pistol.

"Don't move, mister," Jack demanded, as he reached for the handle of the back door on the driver's side.

"All right," Bill responded nervously. "Where's the other guy?"

Jack gritted his teeth at the inquiry. "Don't ask questions. You'll talk when I tell you to." He slid into the rear seat while holding the gun to Bill's head. "Are you familiar with these parts?"

"Yes, I am. You're fairly close to the main road. When you get there you can go right across a big bridge and head away from Grandville or you can go left and it's about 12 miles to town. I seriously doubt if you want to go that way."

Bill could see the livid look on his passenger's face in the rearview mirror and continued, "Listen, why don't you just take my truck and leave me here?"

Jack pondered the offer for a moment and shook his head in refusal. "'Cause I need you for insurance. Now shut up and drive!"

Bill slowly continued, and within less than a quarter of a mile, he looked ahead and saw Joe's new pickup sitting on the left side of the road. Jack recognized the truck as well, and he firmly pressed the end of his pistol into Bill's neck. "Punch it, speed up, go on past that pickup, and don't slow down!"

A few minutes earlier, L.D. had gone to the rear of the truck to wait for Bill's arrival and was leaning on the tailgate, staring at Joe's decomposing 10-pointer and praying for Stan against the danger he was facing. Suddenly, he and Bob heard the roar of the engine as Bill rounded the turn. They were excited to see that their friend had arrived. L.D. laid the pistol on the tailgate and walked to the middle of the road to greet his buddy. As Bill drew closer, Bob noticed he was speeding up.

"L.D., I don't think he's gonna stop!" Bob yelled.

Jack screamed in Bill's ear. "Run over him if you have to!"

"I can't do that, mister!" Bill boldly defied the order and swerved to miss his friend. The quick movement of the large vehicle caused it to lose traction and slide in the gravel, sending Jack flying to the other side of the backseat. The Suburban ended up sitting sideways in the road about 20 yards beyond the confused L.D.

Bill started to jump out of the truck, but Jack was too quick.

"Sit right there or you're a dead man," he commanded.

Bob put the phone down on the front seat, exited Joe's truck, and was about to join L.D. when the right rear door of the Suburban flew open. Deciding he had no other choice than to corral the trio and use them all as hostages, he quickly started barking orders. The two surprised men submitted at the sight of the large gun Jack pointed at their chests. L.D. looked longingly toward Joe's truck where his only weapon of defense was laying on the tailgate.

"You, old man, get in the front seat!" Jack then looked at L.D. with rage in his eyes. "You're that kid's dad, aren't you? Well you'll be happy to know that he's still in good hands with my buddy. Now get in the back and scoot over—and stay on your side!"

Jack climbed in, put the gun to Bill's neck once again, and demanded, "*Now…drive!* And none of you talk unless I tell you to!"

As Bill backed the vehicle up then headed downhill, Joe neared the edge of Six Mile Road. It had taken him longer to get there than he wanted, but he was pleased to be within sight of his truck. He was greeted with two surprises. First, he recognized Bill's green Suburban moving toward him. Then he noticed four figures inside. When he saw Jack holding a pistol to the back of Bill's head, he knew that L.D., Bob, and Bill had been commandeered.

"Oh, no," Joe groaned. He stood motionless as the large truck passed him. His camo allowed him to go undetected. As soon as Bill had gone around the bend, Joe walked forward to get to the edge of the road. That's when he discovered his second surprise.

As he stepped through the tall Johnson grass he tripped on something. When he looked down to maneuver over whatever it was, he was amazed. It was his old friend! His compound bow and the attached quiver full of arrows! After drawing it back and looking it over, he decided it was unharmed and in good working order. He whispered to himself as he looked down the road toward the place he had last seen the Suburban, "Thank You, Lord. At least I'm armed again!"

Matthew gave the turn signal an upward push, guided the mini-van onto Mill Creek Road, and proceeded toward the Gleason farm. Evelyn dug into her purse, found the Carsons' phone, and dialed 911.

"911 operator. How may I assist you?"

"This is Evelyn Tanner. I am inquiring about my husband, Joe Tanner. Trooper Lance Wilson instructed me to check with you."

"Yes, ma'am. Wilson informed us that your husband is returning to his vehicle at this moment. Also, you'll be glad to know the kidnap victim is safely in the hands of one of our troopers."

Evelyn looked up and sighed with relief, then she smiled as she looked at Matthew. He knew she had good news. She continued to listen as the operator added, "It was reported that your husband's truck is on Six Mile Road. Do you know where that is, Mrs. Tanner?"

"Yes, we know. My son and I are headed there right now. Thank you for your help."

Evelyn ended the call and looked at her son with a wide smile. "Matt, I have good news and...I have good news! Stan is safe—*hallelujah!* The other good news is that your dad should be at his truck on Six Mile Road. Let's get there as quickly as we can!"

In the joy of the moment, Matthew looked at his mother and noticed the tears that quietly filled her eyes and her relieved countenance.

Joe hurriedly ran across the road to his truck and found the driver's door still opened. He picked up the phone and looked at the small window on its face. The words *in use* were illuminated. He quickly put the phone to his ear.

"Hello!"

The 911 operator responded, "Yes, Mr. Gleason, I'm still with you."

"Ma'am, this is Joe Tanner!"

"Mr. Tanner?"

"Bob Gleason, L.D. Hill, and Bill Foster are all hostages now. Just as I arrived, they were driving away. The fugitive named Jack had his gun pointed at the back of Bill's head. Tell Trooper Wilson they are headed toward Highway 12. As soon as he can, he should continue down the road he's on; it'll meet with another road, which will lead him to Highway 12."

"I will relay that message right away. Mr. Tanner, I just spoke with your wife. She and your son are on their way to your location. They should be there any moment."

"Oh! Thank you! I'm going to hang up now and wait for them. Thank you so much."

Joe's emotions swirled with joy at the thought of seeing Evelyn and Matthew again. Then he realized what misery his three friends must be feeling. He also thought of the emotional roller-coaster ride Tricia was surely experiencing when she first heard the news of Stan's kidnap, then his return to safety, and now the report of L.D.'s latest predicament. He also knew that Donna would not be left out of the barrage of horrifying emotions when she learned of the predicament Bill was in. In the stillness of the roadside, Joe looked up into the sky and worded a prayer, "We still need You down here, Father!"

23

Earl Potter felt he had waited long enough at the intersection of Mill Creek and Highway 12. He decided to continue on. When he reached the Currey River Bridge, he parked his Chevy at the east end, within sight of Six Mile Road. He remained there just as Trooper Jackson had instructed. As he sat in the stillness of the river area with his window rolled down, he was working through the situation he was in. He was sorry he'd ever agreed to help Jack, and he was also emotionally backpeddling in regard to his decision to face the truth about his past.

Earl wanted desperately to maintain his anonymity in the community he had grown to enjoy, but he assumed his decision to get involved with the police would drastically change his life. He was tempted to drive away from the bridge he was visiting for the fifth time in less than 24 hours. As he struggled with whether or not to hurry to his house, grab a few things, and forever leave Giles County, he saw a large Suburban come to a sliding stop at the end of Six Mile Road.

As the dust roiled up behind the stopped vehicle, Earl put his hand on the ignition key, ready to start his engine. The unfamiliar vehicle turned right and accelerated as it rolled toward him.

When the two vehicles were side by side, Jack looked out the window and got another momentary glimpse of the familiar face he had seen back on Mill Creek Road. He immediately screamed, "Stop the truck! Stop right here!"

Bill smashed down the brake pedal, and all of the men were thrown forward. Jack held his gun tightly in one hand and shoved Bill with the other. "Get out of the truck. All of you get out! Right now!"

Earl was puzzled at the sight in his rearview mirror. The people were suddenly exiting the vehicle that was just behind him. As he watched the scene unfold, he assumed the men were law enforcement who had come to assist the state troopers in capturing Jack and Shelby.

Jack was the last one to exit the Suburban. As he waved his pistol frantically in all directions, Earl couldn't believe his eyes. He quickly started his motor, but before he could drop his Chevy into gear, Jack's gun barrel was in his face.

"Hello there, Tony!"

Bob and L.D. looked at one another and then at Bill. The three of them had never heard Earl referred to as *Tony*. Their curiosity was interrupted when Jack grabbed Earl's door by the handle and forcefully swung it open. "I wanna see your hands, Manzana!" Earl put his hands into the air and sat motionless.

"Why don't you let these guys go, Jack? I'll help you get out of here!" Again, the three friends were amazed. They wondered how Earl knew the suspect's name.

"No way, Tony. We're all gonna get in your hot little Chevy and you're gonna take me to a safer place. I'm gonna need the rest of this bunch for a shield if guns go off!"

Jack walked over behind Bob, put his left arm around his neck, and placed the gun at his temple. "If you don't want to see this old man's lights go out, all of you get into Tony's Chevy."

The group took their seats in the vehicle. Earl was at the wheel, Bob was next to him, then Bill. Jack was in the rear seat on the driver's side across from L.D. He pressed the power button for his window, and when it was fully down he instructed Earl to move in reverse. As the 4x4 rolled backward toward the Suburban, Jack sharply said, "Stop!"

Earl obeyed, bringing the Chevy to a halt next to Bill's Suburban. In one fluid motion, Jack put his pistol out the window, quickly fired two rounds into the radiator, and then pressed the barrel of the gun into L.D.'s ribs.

The four men shook as they watched bright-green fluid pour out of the vehicle. Bill couldn't believe what had just happened; he was so stunned he didn't say a word.

Earl was totally mystified. "Why on earth did you have to do that? We could've taken that truck. It's newer, you know."

"But it's not a four-wheel drive, and we just might need one later. Besides, there'll be plenty of room for just you and me in this thing… in a little while!" Jack's voice angrily growled as he added, "By the way, where were you last night?"

Earl quickly defended himself. "Hey! For your information, Jack, I was at the bridge more than once last night. And listen to this." Earl defiantly pushed the horn on the middle of the steering wheel and held it down for a moment. "Hear that, Jack? It's old, but it still works. Where were you?"

Curiosity got the best of Bob at that moment, and he couldn't hold back the question any longer.

"Do you guys know each other?"

Jack's fury exploded, and he yelled loudly enough that everyone's ears ached at the sound of his voice.

"Don't talk to me. Don't ask me questions. If I want you to know anything, I'll tell you! Drive, Tony." As Earl drove away, Jack worriedly glanced back at the bridge. As he tried to quickly memorize the structure and the surrounding area for future identification, he thought, *I'll be back for my money.*

When Wilson heard the two gun blasts in the distance, he reached for the microphone in Jackson's car and pressed the button.

"Carla, this is Wilson, do you copy?"

"Yes, come back."

"I just heard two gunshots. It sounded like they were about a mile away. When will the other unit be here? We need to send the prisoner back to town so we can check out the gunfire. We can't sit around here very much longer. Where is everybody?"

Carla had good news for Wilson. "One unit is coming out by the river road, another is on the way to your location. A third unit is abandoning a roadblock on the east side of town; it will also be coming your way. We'll dispatch any other units that become available as quickly as possible. And a wrecker is coming for your car."

Trooper Randy Tibbs broke into the communication. "Wilson? Tibbs here. I'm on Mill Creek and just passed what I assume is Six Mile Road. My ETA to your 20 is less than five minutes. Do you copy?"

"10-4, Tibbs. Please hurry. Watch for the sharp curve ahead of you in less than a mile. You'll find my unit there." Wilson was embarrassed to tell him the details. "If you don't take the corner carefully, you'll end up on top of it!" He addressed central again. "Carla, have you spoken with Mrs. Tanner since she entered the area?"

"Negative, Wilson. She was en route the last time we communicated."

As Wilson anxiously watched for Tibbs to arrive, Trooper Jackson entertained Stan with an explanation of all the gadgets and tools of his trade that filled the car in an effort to distract the boy. The observant officer knew the young fellow was worried about his dad. As he handed Stan his handcuffs to examine, Jackson speculated about Earl.

"Wilson, I wonder if Earl Potter is on the up and up. I sure hope he didn't pull the wool over our eyes. He seemed sincere enough to me. How about you?"

Wilson pondered the question as he anxiously looked behind him. "I don't know, Jackson, but I'm with you. If he was fooling us, he did a good job. But if he's on the sly, why would he have chased us down and offered to help? Let's just hope he's on our side."

As Wilson was finishing his sentence, he saw a patrol car coming in the distance. Within moments, he and Jackson exited the car, greeted their friend, and handed the weary prisoner over to him. Stan was grateful to be the front-seat guest of Trooper Tibbs, and he waved thankfully at Wilson and Jackson as the two officers headed to the Currey River Bridge.

"Looks like you've had a pretty exciting day, young man," Tibbs said to Stan, as they climbed into his patrol car.

"Yes, sir. It's one I'll remember for a long time. I sure hope my dad is okay. Do you think he's all right?"

Tibbs saw the aching concern in Stan's face and attempted to offer the young man a bit of comfort. "Well, we'll do our best to get him home safely. We'll also see to it that his truck makes it back to town safe and sound so he can use it again. The wrecker should be here soon. We'll stay here till it does. As for the guy back there," Tibbs pointed at Shelby with his thumb, "he's not goin' anywhere...except to the big house."

As Stan wondered where the "big house" was, he politely smiled, looked out over the dash of the patrol car, and whispered a prayer for his captured father.

Wilson and Jackson pulled onto Highway 12 a few minutes later and turned right. They discovered Bill's ailing Suburban sitting at the end of the bridge, facing west.

"Looks like somebody ought to start a junkyard business out here. This has to be Bill Foster's vehicle. The radiator has been leaking like a broken water main!"

Wilson looked across the bridge, then eastward down the highway. "I wonder where everybody is? Jackson, do you remember what Mr. Potter said about one of the suspects being a relative of his? I have a hunch he might have been sitting right here, just like we told him to be, when Foster's truck came off the hill full of hostages. Unless I miss my guess, that whole bunch is in that white 4x4."

Jackson added his thoughts. "And that empty radiator probably explains the two gunshots we heard a while ago. Let's put the bumper to this truck, get it off the road, and see if we can find them. I suggest we go west a little ways first. I can't imagine the suspect wanting to head back toward Grandville."

Jackson jumped out and got into the Suburban, turned the key to the on position, pressed the brake, and put the gear into neutral. After Wilson pushed the abandoned Suburban to the side of the road and radioed to central for another wrecker to be dispatched to the area, Jackson returned to the patrol car and they cautiously headed west.

Joe had also heard the two shots. As he sat on the driver's side of his truck with the door open and one foot on the ground, he worried about what the gunfire meant. He welcomed the quietness of his surroundings as a momentary reprieve from the chaos of the day he had been having. Suddenly he realized how tired his body was.

"Enough of this adventure," he whispered. "I need to take my 'ticker' home. But I guess this day is a long way from over." As he said the words to himself, he heard the crunching of gravel. His heart raced with excitement when he saw his wife's plum-colored minivan come around the bend. With a wide smile on his face, Joe stepped out of the truck and into the middle of the road.

"Look, Mom, there's Dad!" Matt said with deep relief.

"Oh, my! He sure looks tired and frazzled. And we left home so fast it didn't even dawn on me to bring him something to eat or drink."

Matthew pressed the down button on the window as he carefully drove up to his dad. Joe leaned onto the top of the driver's door with his left hand, and gently put his right hand on Matthew's shoulder. He looked at his son, then sighed deeply as he looked across the van to his bride. "You'll never know how good it is to see you again!"

Evelyn jumped out of the van, ran around to her husband, and gave him a grateful hug. "Are you okay, sweetheart? You look worn out!" Tears of joy filled her eyes as she lovingly patted Joe on his back and felt the sweat-soaked camo shirt squish under her hand.

Joe held Evelyn tightly, then looked at Matt, who was opening the door to join in the embrace. As they enjoyed a family hug, Joe spoke with a faltering voice, "I'm fine, but Bob, L.D., and Bill aren't doin' so well right now. They're being held by one of the gunmen."

24

Joe was tempted to sugarcoat the news about his three friends as he updated Evelyn and Matt on the situation. He struggled to hide the dread in his voice.

"Well, we captured one of the suspects down the hill from where we are right now. He's in custody. Unfortunately, the other guy ran off. He came back up the hill in this direction. I followed him up here, and a few minutes before you drove up, I arrived in time to see Bill drive away with Bob and L.D. in his Suburban. In the backseat was the second culprit. I could see that he had a gun on Bill as they went by me. I'm not sure what to do now!"

Matthew inquired, "Which way did they go, Dad?"

"They went downhill toward the Currey River Bridge."

"Well, let's follow them!"

Joe looked in the direction of the bridge for a long moment, then spoke with a tone of caution. "We've certainly got to help our friends. The fellow who has them hostage probably won't think twice about doin' what he has to do to avoid being captured. His name is Jack. Since he hasn't seen this van, I think we can go down there and see if we can find them. They must be somewhere on Highway 12. Just maybe we can get in sight of the Suburban."

Joe went to the cab of his truck, retrieved his phone, and handed it to Evelyn. "Honey, you operate this thing. Matt, you do the driving, and I'll stay low in the backseat."

"Yes, sir!" Matthew responded with a grateful thumbs up.

"Hang on a minute," Joe announced. There are a couple of things we need to take with us. I'll take my bow and anything else I can find in the truck that we might need. Evelyn, if you will, go to the back of the truck and get my hunting knife out of the orange rubber gloves."

Evelyn stepped to the tailgate and discovered the big buck that was decaying in the warmth of the autumn evening. She sympathetically called out to her husband, "Sure is a nice deer, honey. What a terrible shame for it to go to waste."

Joe looked into the rear window of his truck at his understanding wife and nodded in sad agreement, then continued his search of the cab for other useful items. As Evelyn looked for the gloves, her eyes fell on the .357 that L.D. left behind when Jack had surprised them a few minutes earlier. As she wrapped her hand around the cold pistol and picked it up, she was surprised at how heavy it was.

"Hey, honey, did you know there's a pistol back here?"

Joe joined his wife at the tailgate, and Evelyn handed him the gun. He opened the cylinder and gave it a slow spin. "There are three bullets left, Evelyn, and I have no doubt this belonged to one of those two guys I met up with this morning. L.D. must have found it." Joe handed the revolver back to Evelyn and said, "You remember how to use one of these, don't you?"

"I suspect I do. You taught me well." Her tone of voice hid her reservations.

"If you don't mind, put it in your coat pocket in case we need it," Joe said.

Evelyn's tan-colored, waist-length windbreaker hung slightly crooked under the weight of the gun that filled her pocket. As she walked around the truck to join Joe and Matthew at the minivan, she lightly patted the solid metal lump at her side and mumbled nervously, "If my girls could only see me now!"

Jack took his .357 out of L.D.'s ribs and pushed the barrel into Earl's neck. With his eyes on the other occupants of the Chevy, he waved his sword of intimidation then moved the end of the barrel to the back of Earl's head.

"You'd better cooperate, Tony. 'A mind is a terrible thing to waste,' you know!"

"Take it easy, Jack," Earl soothed. "You've got a good situation here. You have a car full of hostages, and you're the one holdin' all the cards. Just don't get trigger happy on us. We'll get you out of this area. Bob Gleason here knows the roads around these parts like the back of his hand. He can…"

Jack interrupted Earl's speech. "Hey, which one is Gleason?"

Bob held his hand up to identify himself, hoping to generate more conversation. He determined that talk was much healthier than gunfire. "I'm Bob Gleason. Earl and I are neighbors."

Jack paused for a moment. "Earl, huh? Nice name for a Chicago chump. What last name did you steal?"

"Potter. People around here know me as Earl Potter. Now ease up, Jack. Just be calm!"

Jack yelled again, and the sudden outburst reverberated in the small cab. "Don't tell me to be calm. I hate it when people tell me to be calm! I don't see that I have a reason to relax, *Earl!*" Jack said the name with mocking disgust. "I bet there are cops crawling all around here, and I don't want to be calm!"

"Jack, I know Bob can lead us on some back roads to get us over to the interstate."

Bob looked around Bill at Earl with a confident nod. "I can do it, Earl. There's a right turn just ahead and we can go back through the country to Highway 49. That'll take us to the four-lane."

Jack pushed Earl's head into a tilted position with the pistol and looked at Bob. "You'd better be tellin' the truth, old man, or your neighbor will be movin' away for good!"

As Jack was barking his threats, Bob was beginning to mentally plot a course that would lead them back to Highway 12, the only major paved road in that part of Giles County. He knew there was no quicker way to the interstate within 20 miles, other than crossing the Currey River Bridge and heading west, but he figured Jack didn't know it and prayed he would never find out.

As the Chevy 4x4 turned right off the pavement and disappeared into the countryside, Matthew was coming to a halt at the end of Six Mile Road. Evelyn looked to her right and saw the Foster family Suburban sitting just off the highway at the end of the long bridge. "Look! Isn't that Bill's Suburban?"

Matthew pulled the minivan close to the vehicle, and Joe quickly slid the van door open and exited toward the truck. Matthew followed him, and the two walked by the pool of bright-green antifreeze on the road.

"Dad, looks like their new rig's got a bad leak."

Matthew opened the driver's door and popped the hood. Joe examined the radiator and announced, "That explains the two gunshots I heard a few minutes before you found me up on top of the hill. That jerk has put two rounds through the grill. I hope it's only the truck that's been wounded."

Matthew looked around the area. "Well, if they're not here, where in the world did they go?"

Joe shook his head in bewilderment, walked to the back of the empty Suburban, and looked into the cargo area. "Aha! Matt, look what I found!" Joe opened the rear gate and retrieved a crossbow with four bolts mounted in the connected quiver. "Bill got this thing as a birthday gift, and he let me shoot it about two weeks ago. It is an amazing contraption, and it's fast, too. Probably shoots these bolts at more than 300 feet per second. It shoots kind of like a rifle. You just look down the sights and squeeze the trigger. It has a safety, like a gun. We'll take it with us in case we need it!"

Joe wondered if his friends and their captor were nearby on foot or whether another unsuspecting passerby had fallen victim to Jack's desperate attempt to escape. As he climbed back into the van, and was about to direct Matthew to head west, one of the two phones chirped. Joe knew immediately it wasn't his. He was surprised to see Evelyn with another cell phone. As she was answering the call, a different phone came to life. Joe recognized the familiar tone, reached over the seat, and picked up his own.

"Joe Tanner here."

"Mr. Tanner, this is the 911 operator. Where are you at this time?"

As he was explaining his whereabouts, Evelyn was answering her call. "This is Evelyn Tanner."

"Evelyn, this is Tricia Hill. I guess you heard Stan is okay. Praise be to God!"

"Yes, that was wonderful news!" Evelyn happily responded.

"We're on our way toward the Gleason farm. We're not quite to the Mill Creek turnoff."

Evelyn asked, "Who's with you?"

"It's just Donna Foster and me."

"How did you get this number, Tricia?"

When Joe heard Tricia's name, he looked at Evelyn with a questioning stare and then continued his conversation with the 911 operator.

Tricia was grateful to have Evelyn on the line. "I got the number from your industrious daughter Bessie. She was kind enough to agree to watch all of our kids so Donna and I could join in the search for our husbands. When the station called and told us about the predicament they were in, there was no way we could sit around Grandville and not help out. Your girls are the best. Where are you?"

Evelyn dreaded to let Tricia know that only Joe was safe and that he was with her. "Matthew and I are with Joe in our van, sitting at the east end of the Currey River Bridge. Where exactly are you?"

"We're about 11 or 12 miles from you right now, parked along the highway. We had to pull off to get a steady signal on the phone. We'll hurry up and join you there. Will you wait for us?"

"We'll wait. Just be careful!"

"Are Bill and L.D. with you?" Tricia asked.

"No, they're not. I'll explain when you get here."

A few minutes before the two determined wives pulled back onto the highway, Jack started complaining to Earl and Bob. "We've been out here in the boonies much too long. When do you think we're gonna find the hard road again, old man?"

"Actually," Bob answered, "it's just in front of us." His calculated twists and turns on the backroads had managed to sufficiently confuse the gunman, who had been preoccupied with watching the moves of all his captives. He had no idea that the hardtop road Earl was approaching was Highway 12 and that the bridge where Bill's wounded Suburban sat was only a dozen miles away. Bob was keenly aware that if Jack realized they had gone in a big circle and were headed back toward the farm on Mill Creek Road, someone would surely get hurt. Though it was risky and dangerous, Bob was convinced that their welfare was best served by getting back to familiar ground. He gave further instructions.

"Turn left here and stay on this road for about a mile. Then turn right onto the next gravel road." As they turned back toward the Currey River, Bob said a desperate prayer in his heart. *God, we need a miracle here!* Realizing what Bob was up to, his three friends sat quietly in the vehicle and didn't say a word. They simply prayed.

Earl accelerated when they pulled back onto Highway 12, and he quickly reached the speed limit. As he sped around a turn, Bill suddenly stiff-armed the dash and loudly yelled, *"Watch out, Earl!"*

Everyone looked up to see a brownish-colored Honda station wagon pulling onto the highway. Earl hit the brakes and the Chevy began to slide.

When the tires squealed as they skidded over the blacktop, Donna looked in her rearview mirror and saw the fast-approaching vehicle. She knew it wasn't going to stop. *"Hold on, Tricia! We're about to get hit!"*

25

❯❯⟩⟩•⟨⟨❮❮

As Earl's 4x4 plowed into the rear of Donna's Honda, Bob put both of his hands on the dash in front of him to absorb the impact. L.D. was thrown forward. Earl held tightly to the wheel and managed to slow down somewhat before contact. Jack was nearly slammed to his knees, but he recovered quickly and maintained his guard on his hostages.

As the two vehicles sat crunched together in the highway, Bill was mentally processing the unbelievable sight in front of him. It was his wife's car. In the excitement of the chaos, he started to announce the identity of the driver, but quickly decided to let it go unknown. L.D. had noticed the familiar wagon as well, and he shot a quick glance at Bill. With expressions that only longtime friends can read, each of them silently agreed not to say a word.

Jack was resituating himself in the backseat. He nervously shouted, "Back up, Earl, and let's get out of here. This thing is still running. Do it now!"

Earl immediately put his Chevy into reverse and backed away from the Honda. As the two vehicles separated, shattered glass and plastic fell to the pavement. Jack leaned forward and reached around Earl's neck. As he violently choked him, he pushed the hard barrel of the pistol into the back of his head.

"Watch what you're doin', you idiot! I need you to be alert! Now pull around the car and let's go!"

L.D. spoke up. "Don't you think we ought to check on the people in the station wagon?"

"No way," Jack answered. "They're okay. They can deal with it on their own. Just drive, Tony!"

Earl put the Chevy into forward gear and pulled into the oncoming lane to go around Donna's crumpled car.

As they started to go by, Donna said, "Those idiots are gonna drive off! Quick, get a pen and something to write on. Get their plate number!"

Tricia looked into the tray between the two front seats and dug for a pen She opened the glove box to find paper.

As the 4x4 rolled past them, Donna looked out her window at the occupants of the white vehicle and angrily said, "I wanna see the jerks who would do us this way!" She couldn't believe her eyes as she looked over her left shoulder at the faces that were about to go by. "Tricia! Look at this!"

With one hand still in the glove compartment and her body stretched across Donna's lap to see inside the passing vehicle, Tricia saw the faces as they passed and did a double-take. "I do declare. Those 'idiots' just happen to be our husbands!"

As Earl maneuvered around the Honda, Bill was looking out his window. L.D. was staring out his as well, and when the two married couples saw each other behind their walls of glass, they were in total shock. All four pairs of eyes met, and all four jaws were wide open in surprise.

The two women, shaken but uninjured in the crash, gasped in astonishment.

Neither man said a word; they just gawked in amazement. Bob looked around Bill and also got a fleeting glimpse of the two familiar ladies before their worried faces disappeared as the Chevy headed west.

"Quick, Donna, give me the phone!" Tricia requested with her hand out.

Donna handed the phone to her rattled friend like a nurse putting a surgical tool into the hand of a doctor. Tricia punched in the Carsons' phone number and within five seconds heard the first ring.

Evelyn took the chirping phone off the dash of her van and pushed the green button. "Hello, this is Evelyn Tanner."

"Oh, Evelyn! This is Tricia. You're not gonna believe this, but our husbands and Bob Gleason are headed in your direction in a damaged, white Chevy 4x4. Donna says it looks familiar, but we're not sure who's driving. Whoever it was just plowed into the rear of Donna's car and drove away! There was a total of five people crammed into the vehicle."

"Are you two hurt?" Evelyn frantically inquired.

"We're all right. Just totally in shock!"

Evelyn sighed in relief, then quickly relayed the news of the wreck to Joe. He asked for the phone. "Tricia, this is Joe. Let me suggest we hang up, and you call 911 to give your location. Let them know what has just taken place. Also, while you're on the line with the 911 operator, ask them to notify Trooper Lance Wilson of your accident and the Chevy. See if he can come to the Currey River Bridge!"

"Will do," Tricia replied. "It's good to hear your voice, Joe."

"Thank you. Where are you right now, Tricia?"

"Well, we had just pulled back onto the highway when we got rearended. I'm guessing we're about ten minutes from you. I think the car will run. We'll check it out. If we can't move, we'll call you back."

Tricia ended her call and dialed 911.

Evelyn announced to her son and husband that the Chevy full of men was headed their way.

Joe pulled his cap off and ran his hands through his hair. "We've gotta come up with something quick. Our friends are hostages in that vehicle. We can't let it go by us."

Matthew suddenly punched the accelerator of the van and headed east, away from the bridge.

"What on earth are you doing, son?" Joe quickly asked.

"Dad, I have an idea. If that guy thinks he's come up on an accident that is completely blocking the road, he'll have to stop. He hasn't seen this van and won't suspect who it is. You could be out of sight in the cornfield with your bow, and if he gets out of the 4x4, you could..."

Matthew couldn't bring himself to say it in front of his mother, but Evelyn finished the sentence for him. "Shoot him?"

"Yes, ma'am," Matthew said.

Evelyn looked out her window and raised her eyes skyward. "Lord, have mercy on us!"

Joe spoke up and admitted, "It's a great idea, Matt. Let's give it a try, but we've gotta get out of sight of Bill's vehicle."

Matthew drove onto Highway 12 and looked into his rearview mirror to make sure they were out of sight of the Suburban. He checked both directions to be sure there was no other traffic and then made a careful but hasty U-turn. As he pulled sideways in the road to block both lanes, he said, "I'll lie down on the pavement in front of the van, as if I've been hit, and Mom can act like she's tending to me. Dad, you can hide a row or two back in the cornfield." Matthew pointed to the tall, golden-brown stalks of corn that lined the road just a few feet beyond the edge of Highway 12.

As Matthew put the van in park and pushed the emergency brake, Evelyn began digging in the compartment below the radio in the middle of the dash and took out four unused packs of fast-food catsup and held them up. "These might help make it look real."

"Mom! You're a genius! I can use those." Matthew quickly turned to Joe and asked, "Dad, do you have your little knife on you?"

Joe took the knife from his pocket and handed it to his son. An expression of sheepish regret came over Matthew's face as he opened the blade, looked at his mother, and then promptly cut a two-inch slit in his blue jeans on the outer side of his left thigh. Then he ripped a large opening in his shirt. As he squeezed the bloated packages of catsup, he wiped the red paste on his exposed leg, his chest, his face, and his hands. He offered Evelyn an apology. "Sorry, Mom. Gotta make it look real!"

He exited the van and hurried to the front bumper and lay facedown on the hard road with his head and shoulders near the center of the van and his legs protruding out to the side.

Joe grabbed the Carsons' phone and handed it to Evelyn. "Call 911 and ask them to connect you to Trooper Wilson. When you get him, tell him where we are. If the Chevy comes into view, just act like you're really upset—and make it look good. Whatever you do, stay on the line with Wilson. I don't know what's going to happen here today, but I hope the law gets here at the same time our friends do. The guy we're hoping to defeat won't want to stop. You might ask 911 to call Donna and have her halt the traffic that's behind her by parking sideways in the road, just in case Earl Potter is forced to turn around and head back east. I love you, Evelyn!"

She returned a very nervous but sincere smile.

Joe retrieved his bow and started to head toward the cornfield. As he backed out of the van, he glanced at the cargo area and noticed the crossbow. He suddenly got an idea he believed would be a great precaution. He quickly removed it, stepped onto its loading bar, and pulled the string back, locking it into firing position. He nocked a bolt onto the string and checked to see that the safety was on. He walked around to the front of the van and handed the weapon to his son.

"Matt, I'm going to put you in charge of this thing. Use it if you have to, but make sure of what you're shooting. Remember, to shoot it you look down these sights, shove this safety off, and pull the trigger. Keep in mind that this crossbow will shoot level out to 35 or 40 yards. After that, the bolt will start to drop. Aim a little high if it's farther than that."

Matthew shoved the crossbow carefully up under the engine area.

Joe patted Matthew on the shoulder. "Son, you know I always bless the arrows I shoot when I'm in a moment of truth. If you have to pull the trigger on this thing, say a little prayer first. I love you!"

As Joe stood to his feet and brushed his hands off, he heard a firm, "Love you, too, Dad!"

Joe walked across the highway with his bow tucked under his arm. As he eyed the spot he would hide in the autumn corn, Evelyn dialed 9-1-1.

Earl held tightly to the steering wheel of his Chevy, which shook in his hands as a result of the wreck.

Donna was driving her damaged Honda toward the Currey River Bridge.

Wilson reached for the radio mic that hung from its bracket on the patrol car and pressed the button. "Carla, this is Wilson. Any news from Joe Tanner since you spoke with Mrs. Foster about the accident?"

"Yes!" she responded excitedly. "We just got a call from Evelyn Tanner. They are staging an accident just east of the bridge in order to slow down the oncoming vehicle belonging to Earl Potter. She said it contains the hostages, and the suspect is assumed to still be armed."

"Who are *they*?"

"Apparently, Mrs. Tanner and her son are blocking the road. Joe Tanner is with them."

"10-4, Carla. We're on our way. We're a few miles west of the bridge." Wilson radioed for back-up. "Tibbs, what's your 20?"

"We're with the wrecker that's hauling Mr. Hill's pickup, and we're headed down Mill Creek Road. We're about two miles from Highway 12."

Wilson returned with new instructions. "Tibbs, we need more help over here near the Currey River Bridge! I know you have the other suspect and Mr. Hill's son, but we need you to turn right on Highway 12 and come our way. Keep your distance for right now and radio for some help with your passengers. Just be ready to move in at our call. I'll get back to you!"

"10-4, Wilson," Tibbs answered, then he looked over at Stan. "You heard the man, little buddy. Check your safety belt! We're makin' a detour."

Carla broke in. "Central, to car 5."

"Wilson here. Go ahead, central."

"Mrs. Tanner wants to be patched through to you."

"10-4, Carla. I'll hold for Mrs. Tanner."

Thirty seconds later, Wilson heard the anxious voice of Evelyn Tanner. "Trooper Wilson, I'm glad I've got you on the line. Do you know what's going on out here?"

"Yes, I do. We're moving as fast as we can to your location."

"That's good, Lance," Evelyn said, then added, "Donna Foster is behind us. Can you contact her and ask her to block the road? That way we don't have to worry about someone hitting us."

"Yes, ma'am. I'll do it now. Don't hang up."

Wilson juggled his conversations, and Evelyn could hear him as he expertly relayed the messages to his communications base in Grandville.

Evelyn looked around the van toward the east, and all was quiet... at the moment.

Then Matthew spoke up from his prone position on the hard road. "Mom, if I have to use this crossbow, make sure you're out of the way!"

Evelyn leaned down and looked up under the van at the weaponry that waited within arm's reach of her son. When she stood back up she felt the heavy gun in her coat pocket as it swayed back to her side with a gentle thump. As she held the cell phone to her ear and waited on hold, she whispered a short, but desperate prayer. "Oh, God, do have mercy on us!"

About eight miles east of the Tanner van that sat in the middle of Highway 12, Earl was preparing to turn right onto Mill Creek as Bob had instructed. At the sight of the graveled road, Jack decided to take over the job of issuing directions. "Tony...just stay on the paved road. With the shape this hunk of junk is in, we don't need to take a ride on a washboard."

Bob challenged the decision in fear of what would happen if Jack saw the familiar bridge again. "I don't recommend that route, mister. That'll get you nothin' but trouble!"

Jack angrily slapped the elderly gentleman on the side of his head with his open hand. "Shut up, ole man. I'm in charge here. Just keep goin', Earl, and step on it!" Bill started to retaliate, but the distinct sound that the hammer of a pistol makes when it's pulled back motivated him to change his mind. Everyone sat stunned and quiet as the Chevy lumbered toward the Currey River Bridge. Jack carefully released the hammer.

26

The highway was uncommonly quiet as Joe stepped into the third row of the tall, mature corn and dropped to one knee. He nocked an arrow, removed his shooting tab from his shirt pocket, and put it on his fingers. The van was in view, but because of the cornstalks, he couldn't see very well beyond the front of the van. In the stillness, he could see Evelyn as she knelt in preparation for her theatrics. The minutes that passed seemed like hours to the three family members.

"Evelyn, are you still with me?" Wilson asked.

"I'm still here. Where are you?"

"We're about seven miles west of the bridge on Highway 12. Tell me what you see."

"Well, strangely enough, I am kneeling over my son at this moment, who is lying halfway underneath the bumper of my van."

Wilson's voice revealed shock. "What!"

"It's okay, Lance. It's part of the plan. If that Chevy 4x4 comes our way, it'll have to stop. We've just staged an accident involving a pedestrian. We've blocked the road completely. Joe's over in the..."

Evelyn stopped in midsentence to listen.

Joe's ears became radarlike as he and Evelyn simultaneously heard the distant low roar of a vehicle coming their way. Joe wrapped the finger tab around the string.

"Speak to me, Evelyn," Wilson ordered.

With the phone still to her ear, Evelyn peered over the hood of the van and looked through the clear front and rear glass. Her voice was shaking. "It's the white Chevy! I can see it through the windows! You better get here as quickly as you can!"

Wilson checked his seat belt and said to his partner, "Faster, Jackson, things are about to unravel on the other side of the bridge! We've got citizens involved in this mess, and it's too late to call them off." Jackson punched the accelerator as Wilson continued. "Evelyn, keep talking to me. What do you see?"

"The vehicle is slowing down. He's slowing way down!"

"Just keep playing your part. Make it look good."

"Well, that may not be so hard to do!"

As Earl slowed his Chevy, the voice behind him boomed in his ear, "Good grief, what now?" Jack's breath was putrid as he sighed deeply in disgust. "This is all I need!"

"Looks like someone's been run over," Earl said as he crept slowly toward the van.

Earl steered as far left as he could and saw the body on the road. Then he announced, "Oh! Looks like it's a kid! And he's really bloody!"

L.D., Bill, and Bob were horrified at the sight, and their hearts sank in despair when they recognized Evelyn. They noticed she had a phone to her ear and appeared to be in great anguish. Each of them felt completely helpless and frustrated, knowing they were at the mercy of a madman.

Jack grabbed Earl by the neck with his left hand and dug his dirty fingernails into his skin. "Just go on around this mess. Don't you even think about stoppin' this time!"

"Hey, Jack! I'm not sure there's room. And we've gotta help this lady and that poor kid. Look at the blood on his face. At least you could let one of us out to help, and the rest of us will go on with you. You've got plenty of shields—you can spare one of us. Have a heart for once, Jack!"

The gruesome sight of the woman kneeling over the injured young-ster managed to touch Jack somewhere in his cold heart. Everyone in the Chevy was surprised when he instructed Earl to pull off in front of the van and then looked at Bill. "You—when we stop up ahead, get out and help that woman and the kid. If you wanna see your friends alive again, you'll forget you ever saw me!"

Earl moved the Chevy at a snail's pace around the scene and stopped about 25 yards in front of the van. As Bill got out of the 4x4, Joe slowly stood up, stepped forward to the edge of the corn, and came to full draw. Bill exited alone. As Joe put his 40-yard pin just above the left rear tire he whispered, "Get out of that Chevy, *Mr. Jack*! I dare you!"

Bob slid over to the far side of the 4x4 and, as he closed the door, Joe decided it was time to take action. Hoping to deflate a tire and force Jack out into the open, he let the string slide off his fingers and sent the arrow on its way. Sparks flew on the pavement as the arrow sailed underneath the white Chevy, missing the tire by two inches and skip-ping into the weeds on the other side of the road.

As Joe was quickly removing another arrow from his quiver and placing it on the string, Matthew reached for the crossbow and pulled it to his shoulder. He shoved the safety off and, without hesitating, put the left rear tire of the Chevy in the sights. Just before he squeezed the trigger, he whispered, "God, bless this arrow!"

The 18-inch shaft catapulted from the bow and rocketed toward the rear of Earl's vehicle. From Matthew's angle close to the ground, the bolt rose slightly and completely missed the tire and flew to the right. It loudly pierced through the lower portion of metal that was exposed below the bumper.

Joe was happily astonished when he heard the bolt connect with the Chevy, and said a firm, "Yes!"

In the same moment, Matthew saw what the bolt had done and whispered a desperate, "*No!*"

Jack was stunned by the sudden thump. "What the…What was that?"

"Must be somethin' caused by the wreck," Earl suggested as he stomped the brake pedal.

Within moments, the strong smell of gasoline filled the vehicle. L.D. said in horror, "It's the gas tank! We've gotta get out of here! One spark and we'll all fry!"

Suddenly Jack opened his door and backed out of the Chevy without taking his gun off the passengers. He commanded them to remain inside. Earl was tempted to take the chance to drive away, but because of the fear of somehow igniting the gas and also not wanting to leave Joe's family to deal with his unpredictable ex-in-law, he turned his motor off and sat still in the road.

Jack slammed the door shut and stepped away from the vehicle that was losing a gallon of fuel every 30 seconds. The road around him was wet with gasoline. He noted that the stream of fuel running down the pavement resembled a fuse to a bomb. He hadn't noticed, however, that Matthew had come to life, and he didn't see Joe in the cornfield. His focus was on the deadly idea that came to him when he saw the "fuse" in the road. It was his chance to destroy everyone who could identify him.

With a devilish look, Jack walked back from the tailgate. With one hand, he reached into his pants pocket, pulled out a dollar bill, and put it between his teeth. He pressed it between his thumb and index finger and pulled it until it was fully extended. Then, with the same hand, he retrieved a cigarette lighter from his shirt pocket.

With Jack only about 30 yards from his position in the corn, Joe nocked another arrow and once again came to full draw. As Jack lit the dollar bill that he held in his teeth, Joe put his sights on the suspect's calf and released the string. Jack screamed in pain as the broadhead ripped through his denim pants and sliced through his leg, severing the muscle in his lower right calf. As he fell to the pavement, the pistol flew out of his hand and into the dirt and gravel at the edge of the road. The flaming dollar bill lilted downward like a falling leaf, and when it landed on the pavement, the gasoline ignited.

Earl was watching the scene unfold behind him and screamed, "Bail out!"

Three doors flew open. L.D. helped Bob as the two of them ran and tumbled into the brush. Evelyn and Matthew, along with Bill, took cover behind the van. Earl made a near-fatal mistake of taking an extra second to grab his wallet under his seat. At the last microsecond, he jumped away just as the Chevy's gas tank exploded, sending an intense wall of heat in all directions. The sound of the blast was deafening as the mushroom of yellow and red flames shot skyward.

As the white 4x4 was turning into an ugly black heap of charred ruins, Jack held his bleeding calf in his hands and scooted toward his pistol. When he was about three feet from retrieving it and attempting to take charge of the scene again, he suddenly saw a foot kick the gun another five feet down the road. When he turned to face the person responsible, he was surprised to hear a female voice say, "Don't move, mister, or I'll put a hole in your other leg. And if that doesn't work, I'll drown you in this stuff!"

Joe couldn't believe his eyes as he quickly walked back onto the highway toward his wife. There was Evelyn, standing over Jack in a policelike stance, holding the silver .357 in one hand and a familiar can of mace in the other. Both weapons were pointed directly at the seriously wounded suspect.

Jack moaned and turned over on his back, only to see a circle of people gathering around him like wolves at a fresh caribou carcass. Earl looked at the pitiful, bleeding, and scorched enemy who lay on the road. "Looks like you're surrounded, Jack!"

"Get me some help, Tony. I'm gonna bleed to death!"

Evelyn took her stare off Jack for a moment and gave Earl a puzzled look. As he removed his belt to use as a tourniquet, Earl returned a glance that implied, "I'll explain later."

In the distance, as the sound of a siren grew louder, Earl taunted the captive. "Looks like you're gonna have all the help you'll ever need in just a few minutes, Jack!"

"You're goin' down with me on this one, Tony!"

"I don't know about that, Jack," Bob said as he took the belt from Earl and began to wrap it around Jack's leg. "Earl has an alibi. He was with me yesterday evening. About the time you and your buddy were terrorizing Grandville, Earl and me were havin' some conversation in my front yard. I can vouch for him. And by the way, I'm really glad you took over as navigator back there." With his farm-callused hands, Bob cinched the belt painfully tight around Jack's wounded leg.

As his former brother-in-law writhed in pain, Earl took the timely opportunity to dig through Jack's pockets and found a small black book. He tucked it safely into his shirt and said, "I don't think you'll need this anymore." Jack offered little resistance to Earl's search and could only beg for medical assistance.

Joe stood by and was in shock by all that had happened. As he surveyed the carnage, Matthew was wiping the last of the catsup off his face and approaching his dad. He put his arm around his father's shoulder, looked in Jack's direction, and, with a tone of sympathy, offered a sincere compliment. "Good shot, Dad!"

"Thanks! And…same to you, Matt."

"Well, the gas tank is not where I aimed, but at least I connected."

Joe gave his son a high-five.

Matthew added, "Dad, I've gotta tell you, after I took the shot, and as I was watching everything unfold in front of me, I thought of the psalm I've heard you quote often. 'For I will not trust in my bow.' I think I know who guided that arrow. I'm glad *He* was here with us!"

"Me, too!" Joe hugged Matthew tightly and peered over his son's shoulder in the direction of his wife. "Son, look at your mother. She sure is a sight, isn't she?"

Joe and Matthew smiled as they looked at Evelyn, still standing over Jack with her weapons pointed at him.

L.D. stepped to Evelyn's side and offered, "Would you like me to take over, Officer Tanner?"

"Please do, L.D.!" Evelyn answered as she handed the gun to the one person in the crowd who wanted most to have the suspects at gunpoint. When Joe saw the vengeful way L.D. looked at Jack, it suddenly dawned on him that his weary comrade had yet to hear the good news about his son. With an indescribable joy in his heart, Joe put his arm around his friend's shoulder.

"L.D., Stan is okay. You're not gonna believe what your brave boy did to help us capture the other suspect. He sure has a great story waiting to tell you. Your son is safe!"

The relief in L.D.'s face was obvious as tears formed in his eyes. He nearly collapsed in relief as he motioned for Bill to come and relieve him of the pistol. He was grateful that the desire for revenge that raged in his heart was suddenly leaving.

Joe then addressed his wife as he put his arm around her to support her, "That was pretty impressive, Evelyn. You still surprise me, honey!"

L.D. waved both of his hands in front of him as if to give the "wait a minute" signal and then stepped squarely in front of Joe. As he had been known to do when a buddy harvested a deer, L.D. did his usual mock-bowing routine, and said, "I saw your buck up there layin' behind your truck. Man, what a monster."

Joe chuckled as L.D. continued, "You did some mighty fancy shootin' today, buddy, and apparently a lot of it. How are your shoulders?"

To show his regrets, Joe pursed his lips and slowly shook his head from side to side. "My shoulders aren't half as sore as this guy's leg and his buddy's arms are gonna be tomorrow. I tell you, L.D., it's really a strange feeling to have a human in the peep sight!"

"Well, buddy, if it makes you feel any better, a lot of us are glad you were able to get the string back as many times as you did."

Evelyn smiled, walked behind Joe, and started massaging his shoulders. "Don't worry about Joe's muscles, L.D., it's his brain that might swell up when we take what's left of that big buck back to town."

27

⊳━◆━○━◆━⊲

As daylight began to fade into darkness, Trooper Jackson pulled his patrol car up to the smoldering scene and, along with Wilson, quickly exited. They both drew their weapons out of their holsters and held them upright as they approached the crowd that had gathered around the captured suspect.

"Step aside, folks. Thank you!" Wilson said. He looked at the pool of blood on the pavement from Jack's wounded leg.

Bob looked proudly at Wilson. "Well, there's your other man. You won't be needin' those pistols, and you have the Tanners to thank for him layin' here on the road waitin' for you!"

Bill spoke up and complimented his elderly friend. "Oh sure, Bob. How about that little trip we took around the mulberry bush with this guy? That was a brilliant delay tactic. I was as lost as a goose back on some of those roads. I had no idea where you were taking us."

"Looks like we have a lot of folks to thank for this fellow being in custody," Trooper Wilson said, as he holstered his gun and cuffed Jack's hands behind his back. "We need to get him to the hospital. Then he'll join his buddy for the ride back to Chicago. What a nasty wound in this guy's leg!"

Joe admitted, "I'm responsible for that. All I had was my three-blade

231

broadheads. When I saw he was about to incinerate my friends, I did what I had to do."

Trooper Jackson grimaced at Joe's description of the devastating implement and shook his head in pity when he imagined the pain Jack was feeling. As they helped him off the blacktop, another car pulled up behind Evelyn's van. Bill could see it was Donna's crumpled Honda, and he smiled as he handed the .357 to Bob and ran toward his wife. Tricia got out and hurried to L.D.'s arms. The two couples lovingly embraced.

Donna dug through her pants pockets, looking for tissue to wipe her eyes. "We could see the smoke a long way off, and we just had to come and see what happened. Is everybody okay, Bill?"

"Yep, except for the fellow who's handcuffed and bleeding from his leg. They're takin' him to Giles Memorial. His buddy, I understand, has two holes in his body, thanks to Joe's fine archery skills. Then there's Joe's truck sittin' up on the hill on Six Mile that won't start; L.D.'s truck has new air conditioning; I hear that Wilson's car is takin' a nap in the turn at Seven Mile; our 'Burban is bleedin' antifreeze; and our Honda is havin' serious back pains. Mr. Gleason's noggin got rattled, and Earl's Chevy went out in a blaze of glory. Other than that…everything's fine."

As Bill continued his uniquely Southern-styled account of the evening's adventure, another patrol car was coming onto the scene. It parked behind the Honda. Stan jumped out and ran to L.D. and Tricia. The three of them formed a happy bundle of family at the road's edge. L.D.'s eyes once again started to swim in joyous tears as he said, "Hallelujah to the name of the Lord who has brought us together again!" Stan looked tenderly into his dad's watery eyes and smiled. "Caught us a couple of big ones today, huh, Dad?"

Trooper Tibbs found Wilson wrapping first-aid gauze around Jack's wound. He said, "Lance, I just talked to central, and I have some good news and bad news. The good news is they believe Phillip Simpson is going to make it. Unfortunately your father-in-law had a heart attack, and they found him just a little while ago in his kitchen. First reports are that when they got to him he was mumbling something about having been attacked and his truck stolen last night. He said he can identify the two men who beat him up at gunpoint. He's recovering at Memorial. And if I know Harold Scutter, he'll be just fine."

Wilson stopped his emergency medical attention and looked into Jack's eyes. His prisoner stared back with an empty look, void of any sorrow.

Tibbs continued. "When the call came in about Harold, my prisoner got really nervous. I guess adding car theft to his record was the straw that broke the criminal's back, 'cause he started to talk. He said it was this guy who masterminded the whole affair, and he wants a separate ride back to Chicago. I know that's a ridiculous request, but I took the liberty of using it to bargain a little with him. In exchange for the promise of isolation from his buddy, I found out about a couple of items these guys stashed that we'll need to retrieve. For one, your father-in-law's old truck is below the bridge at the bottom of the river."

At that news, Wilson was tempted to "accidentally" close the door on Jack's leg, but he forced himself to control his anger. As he stood up, Tibbs added, "The other item we need to recover will be a little easier. The money from the robbery is tucked up under the bridge. And I have no doubt whatsoever that the Harper family will be pleased to hear about it."

The traffic that was piling up behind the emergency vehicles, wreckers, and a clean-up crew included a lot of onlookers. As Joe stood gazing at the sight, he realized he still had his camo on and that he was still holding his bow. He decided he probably looked a little strange to those who were walking onto the scene, so he stepped to the minivan to put his bow away and remove his face paint. As he did, he noticed that the patrol car behind the Honda still had a quiet occupant locked inside.

Joe found Trooper Tibbs. "Would you do me a favor? Would you check your prisoner's pockets and see if you can find a truck part on him? I believe he has something that might restore the heartbeat to my vehicle."

Tibbs returned within a few minutes and handed Joe the ignition coil wire that he'd found in Shelby's coat pocket. "The prisoner wants you to know that he won't forget you."

Joe smiled. "You tell him for me that I'll not forget the bullet shower he gave me this morning. And tell him I'm sorry I had to poke holes in him. Really, I am."

Evelyn listened to Joe's comments and stared at him with shock on her face. "Just how many times did you shoot at someone today, Robin Hood?"

Having been referred to by that ancient name earlier in the day in a not-so-pleasant moment, Joe chuckled out loud. "I lost track, Evelyn. Let me just put it this way. I'll be doing some shopping for a dozen more arrows as soon as I can."

Evelyn smiled. "I think you deserve them."

As Bob unloaded the .357 that Bill had handed him, he walked over to his young neighbor. "Earl, I've got to know just one thing."

Earl knew what question was coming as he leaned on the hood of the Tanner van.

"How is it that this fellow, Jack, knew your name? Are you involved in this craziness somehow?"

"No, sir. I had nothing to do with what happened at Harper's store last night. The only connection I have to all of this is that Jack is my former brother-in-law. He knows a not-so-great part of my past that I haven't told anyone around here about."

In an effort to offer Earl the freedom to say—or not say—more about his history, Bob responded with understanding. "Well, if you ever need anyone to jaw with about all that, I have an available ear." Earl looked at his elderly friend in the way a son would look at a gracious father.

Trooper Wilson joined the two men at the hood of the van. "Mr. Potter, we've gotta get to Giles Memorial with the ambulance, but before I go, I wanted to say thanks for your help today. Please call me tomorrow. I'll need anything else you can add to our files about these two guys. Feel free to call anytime. You know where to find me."

Earl paused to gather his thoughts and to drink in the unexpected blessing of the trooper not pressing him about his past. Grateful for the trust that was being shown to him, he respectfully said, "Sorry about your patrol car, Trooper Wilson. I'm happy I could be of service to you today. You'll never know how glad I am!"

Bob held out both hands and with open palms presented the pistol and remaining rounds of ammunition to Wilson. "I'm sure you'd like to have these items, my friend."

"Yes, Bob, and thank you."

Bob's seasoned wisdom clearly showed as he added, "Trooper Wilson, today was obviously out of the ordinary for all of us. I know the police don't encourage citizens to get actively involved in helping round up outlaws. But people around here love each other in a way that makes me proud. You've got to hand it to these men's wives. Evelyn, Donna, and Tricia are like protective she-bears when it comes to their families. They're not gonna stand around and let the wolves take over. And their kids, especially Stan and Matthew, discovered a lesson today about the kind of courage most children will never get a chance to learn."

Wilson nodded his head in an understanding way as Bob continued. "I just want to say thanks to you and all your police buddies for letting us help...whether you wanted us to or not. But to be honest, I'm not sure you could've stopped it. I think we're all happy things turned out the way they did."

Trooper Wilson extended his right hand toward Bob. "Mr. Gleason, let me shake the hand of a man who survived the most memorable day I have had as a trooper. And to be perfectly honest, I hope nothing else ever tops it!"

As Wilson walked away, Earl's facial expression showed his awe of the exchange he had just witnessed. "Mr. Gleason, I'm not sure what I did to end up in this county, but from the depths of my heart I must say I'm glad I did." Earl deeply sighed. Suddenly, two of the words in the trooper's statement of thanks to him echoed loudly in his mind— *feel free*. No sweeter words could have been said, especially from a representative of the law. Before he could change his mind, he turned to his neighbor and said, "Bob, I barely escaped a fiery death today."

Bob agreed. "Yes, sir, that was a mighty close call!"

Earl shuffled his feet, looked toward his smoldering 4x4, and added,

"Since this fiasco started last night, I've been thinking a lot about some things you and Sarah have told me more than once over the past four years. You know, things like 'getting all cleaned up inside, and ready for heaven.'"

Bob put his hands in his pockets, looked down at the pavement, and enjoyed the warmness in his heart that always came at the mention of Sarah's name. He nodded his head in an understanding way as Earl continued.

"She told me one time about another type of fire I needed to escape. Can we go to your house tonight and talk about that a little more?"

"Earl, I'd like nothing better than to end this day on a positive note. And having you at my table for a late-night cup of hot coffee and some chicken sandwiches would sure be a blessing. And..." Bob paused and thought of how much he wished Sarah could have been there to hear the young man's request. "Before the day is over, I guarantee that from now on you won't have to worry about any more fires."

Trooper Tibbs headed to the bridge with Shelby, who would direct him to the duffel bag before being taken to the emergency room. Jack was already being transported to the hospital.

With his friends preparing to make their way home in patrol cars and wreckers, Joe set about to gather his family. He hated to interrupt Matthew's energetic and enjoyable conversation with Stan, but he called to his son. "Let's go, Matt. You can drive us to my pickup."

As Joe and Matthew climbed into their van, Evelyn was ending her call informing the girls of the outcome of the day. She glanced at Joe with a sympathetic look and offered her tired husband an idea that was sure to console him. "Dear, the head and rack on that buck that's laying up there on the hill sure would look good over the fireplace."

Joe knew that spot in their home was reserved for special items that blended with an elegant décor. Upon hearing Evelyn lovingly concede to the idea of hanging a head mount above the mantel and knowing she was aware of the cost of taxidermy, Joe said a sincere, "Thank you, sweetheart. Thank you so much!"

As they drove away, he thought about Evelyn's gracious offer. Then another idea came to his mind. "You know, honey, I appreciate your suggestion, but if it's all right with you, there's a little market on the east end of town where I'd like to hang that deer. I have a feeling that my buck is a distant relative of the big one that's already hangin' there."

Through You we will push back our
adversaries; through Your name we
will trample down those
who rise up against us.
For I will not trust in my bow,
nor will my sword save me.
But You have saved us from
our adversaries, and You have put to
shame those who hate us.
In God we have boasted
all day long,
and we will give thanks to Your name forever.

PSALM 44:5-7

Notes

Chapter 1—We'll See Him Again

1. Steve Chapman, "We'll See Him Again," Times & Seasons Music/BMI, 2013. Used by permission. All rights reserved.

Chapter 5—Tangled Web

1. Steve Chapman, *A Look at Life from a Deer Stand Devotional* (Eugene, OR: Harvest House Publishers, 2009), chap. 64, "The Web."

2. Steve Chapman, "The Tangled Web," Times & Seasons Music/BMI, 2009. All rights reserved. Used by permission.

Chapter 6—An Obsession

1. Steve Chapman, "Faithfully Follow You," Times & Seasons Music/BMI, 2013. All rights reserved. Used by permission.

Chapter 7—Bullets and Believers

1. Clara McAlister Brooks, "One in Christ," 1911, http://www.hymnary.org/text/as_sweet_strains_of_heavenly_music, accessed 1/28/14.

Chapter 8—He Cares

1. Frank E. Graeff, "Does Jesus Care," 1901, http://www.hymntime.com/tch/htm/d/o/e/doesjeca.htm, accessed 9/18/13.

Chapter 9—Start Counting

1. Steve Chapman and Lindsey Williams, "I'm Countin' on Him," Times & Seasons Music (BMI) Really Big Bison Productions (SESAC), 2013. All rights reserved. Used by permission.

Chapter 10—While You Were Away...

1. Steve Chapman, "Acres of Diamonds," Times & Seasons Music/BMI, 2012. All rights reserved. Used by permission. This lyric was adapted from a story titled "Acres of Diamonds," by Russell H. Conwell, founder of Temple University in Philadelphia, PA. The story was published in 1890 by The John Y. Huber Company, Philadelphia, PA.

If you liked Steve Chapman's

The Tales Hunters Tell,

you're sure to enjoy

A Look at Life from a Deer Stand!

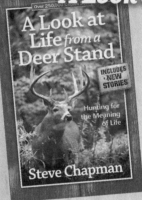

Great Outdoor Adventures

From the incredible rush of bagging "the big one" to standing in awe of God's magnificent creation, Steve Chapman invites you to join him on his forays into the heart of deer country. Discover how the skills necessary for great hunting can help you draw closer to God, improve relationships, and achieve success.

"*A Look at Life from a Deer Stand* is the story of a life journey with God walked through a hunter's woods. Written with artistry and sensitivity for life, it is a joy to read."

LOWELL THILL, vice-president
Christian Bowhunters of America

"*A Look at Life from a Deer Stand* should be mandatory reading for every deer hunter in America. It's that good!"

CHARLES J. ALSHEIMER, field editor
Deer and Deer Hunting Magazine

"*A Look at Life from a Deer Stand* will bring back fond memories for every reader who is a hunter, from the first deer to the last. More importantly, however, it puts in proper perspective our relationship with nature, our friends, our family, and ultimately, with the One who created the magnificent white-tailed deer."

BRAD HERNDON, wildlife photographer,
author of *Mapping Trophy Bucks*

"*A Look at Life from a Deer Stand* has a warm, honest, and humorous spirit that will keep you totally captivated until you turn the last page."

PAUL MEEKS, CEO of Great Day, Inc., and
founder of API Outdoors, Inc.

ALSO AVAILABLE

A Look at Life from a Deer Stand Study Guide
A Look at Life from a Deer Stand Gift Edition